J. Goldina

CW00970513

Rules
for I
Distributors 2014

Free Pharmaceutical Press

e-alerts

Our latest product news *straight to your inbox*
register@ **www.pharmpress.com/alerts**

Pharmaceutical Press is the publishing division of the Royal Pharmaceutical Society

Rules and Guidance for Pharmaceutical Distributors 2014

Compiled by the Inspection, Enforcement and Standards Division of the MHRA

Pharmaceutical Press

Published by Pharmaceutical Press

1 Lambeth High Street, London SE1 7JN, UK

© Crown Copyright 2014

Medicines and Healthcare
Products Regulatory Agency

MHRA, a centre of the Medicines and Healthcare Products Regulatory Agency
151 Buckingham Palace Road
Victoria
London SW1W 9SZ
Information on re-use of crown copyright information can be found on the MHRA
website: www.mhra.gov.uk

Designed and published by Pharmaceutical Press 2014

(**PP**) is a trade mark of Pharmaceutical Press

Pharmaceutical Press is the publishing division of the Royal Pharmaceutical Society

First edition published in 2007

Typeset by OKS Group, Chennai, India
Printed by Berforts Information Press, Eynsham, Oxford
Index Provided by Indexing Specialists, Hove, UK.

ISBN 978 0 85711 102 9 (print)
ISBN 978 0 85711 147 0 (eBook)

All rights reserved. No part of this publication may be reproduced, stored in a retrieval
system, or transmitted in any form or by any means, without the prior written
permission of the copyright holder.
   The publisher makes no representation, express or implied, with regard to the
accuracy of the information contained in this book and cannot accept any legal
responsibility or liability for any errors or omissions that may be made.
   Website listings published in this guide other than www.mhra.gov.uk are not under
MHRA control, therefore we are not responsible for the availability or content of any
site. Listings should not be taken as an endorsement of any kind and we accept no
liability in respect of these sites.
   A catalogue record for this book is available from the British Library.

Contents

Preface to the 2014 edition

In 2007, the MHRA published Rules and Guidance for Pharmaceutical Distributors 2007, as a separate guide for distributors who do not require the elements of the Rules and Guidance for Pharmaceutical Manufacturers Distributors 2007 (the "Orange Guide") which examines Good Manufacturing Practice. Rules and Guidance for Pharmaceutical Distributors 2007, reproduced those elements of the Orange Guide, on the wholesale supply and distribution of medicines for human use, essential to safeguard public health.

Since the 2007 edition there have been significant changes and additions to the detailed European Community guidelines on Good Distribution Practice (GDP) as well as substantial amendments to the Community code relating to medicinal products for human use. This new edition of Rules and Guidance for Pharmaceutical Distributors covers these important changes and features the revised EU Guide for good distribution practice, revisions to the EU Directive on medicines for human use and new chapters for brokers of finished medicines and manufacturers, importers and distributors of active substances as a result of Falsified Medicines Directive 2011/62/EU. In addition this revised guide contains updated chapters on the work of the MHRA, extracts from the UK's consolidated human medicines legislation and a new appendix of names and addresses of other EU medicines regulators. Some references relating to the requirements affecting manufacturers of finished medicinal products and manufacturers of active substances have been specifically included in order to ensure awareness.

Changes to the Community Code

The Falsified Medicines Directive 2011/62/EU amends Directive 2001/83/EU in a number of places. The first tranche of these changes in relation to manufacturing, wholesale dealing, supervision and sanctions come into force from 2 January 2013 with others relating to the importation of active substances from countries outside of the EEA taking effect from the 2 July 2013. Several other requirements, such as the matters relating to safety features, are likely to take longer to transpose as they rely on additional regulations and guidance from the European Commission. These provisions are implemented in the United Kingdom by regulations amending the Human Medicines Regulations 2012.

The headline changes are as follows:

- The current regulatory expectation for the manufacturer of the medicinal product to have audited their suppliers of active substances for compliance with the relevant Good Manufacturing Practice ("GMP") has been formalised, as is the requirement for the written confirmation of audit (the "QP Declaration", currently required as part of the Marketing Authorisation application). This audit may be undertaken by the manufacturer of the medicinal product, or by a suitable and appropriately experienced third party under contract to the manufacturer of the medicinal product.
- In addition a formal requirement for manufacturers of medicinal products (or a third party acting under contract) to audit their suppliers of active substances for compliance with the requirements of Good Distribution Practice ("GDP") particular to active substances has also been introduced.
- A new requirement for manufacturers, importers and distributors of active substances to be registered with the Competent Authority of the Member State in which they are established (in the UK this would be the MHRA). Registrations will be entered onto a database operated by the European Medicines Agency, in a similar manner to the EudraGMP database. The manufacturer of the medicinal product must verify that their suppliers of active substances are registered.
- The regulatory expectation that manufacturers of the medicinal product will verify the authenticity and quality of the active substances and excipients they use has been formalised.
- The manufacture of active substances for use in a licensed medicinal product must be in compliance with the relevant GMP. These standards are currently described in Part II of the EU Guidelines on Good Manufacturing Practice.
- Active substances imported from outside of the EEA must have been manufactured in accordance with standards of GMP at least equivalent to those in the EU and from the 2 July 2013 must be accompanied by a written confirmation that equivalent GMP standards and supervision apply in the exporting country, unless the active substance is sourced from a country listed by the European Commission or exceptionally and where necessary to ensure availability of medicinal products an EU GMP certificate for the site of manufacture is available.

- Manufacturers of medicinal products are required to assess the risk to product quality presented by any excipients they use, by way of a formalised documented risk assessment, and ascertain the appropriate good manufacturing practices necessary to assure their safety and quality. There is no explicit obligation for the medicinal product manufacturer to audit their suppliers of excipients, but it does require the manufacturer to assure themselves that the appropriate good manufacturing practices are being applied.
- In support of the above changes the European Commission is to adopt the following by means of delegated acts and guidelines:
  - principles and guidelines for GMP for active substances;
  - GDP guidelines for active substances; and
  - guidelines for the formal risk assessment process for excipients.
- New obligations on medicinal product manufacturers, wholesale distributors and brokers to inform the Competent Authority and Marketing Authorisation Holder ("MAH") should information be obtained that products either manufactured under the scope of the manufacturing authorisation or received or offered may be falsified, whether those products are being distributed through the legitimate supply chain, or by illegal means.
- The introduction of the concept of brokering for finished medicinal products and associated obligations to comply with the applicable aspects of GDP.
- A new requirement for persons undertaking the wholesale distribution of medicinal products to third countries to hold an authorisation and to check that their customers are authorised to receive medicines. Where the medicinal products for export have been imported from a third country checks must also be made to ensure the supplier is authorised to supply medicines.
- An extension of the requirement to notify the MHRA and the MAH where a wholesale dealer imports from another EEA Member State into the UK a medicinal product which is the subject of a Marketing Authorisation, and the importer is not the MAH or acting on the MAH's behalf, to centrally authorised products (those holding a Marketing Authorisation granted by the European Medicines Agency), and the introduction of the option for the Competent Authority to charge a fee for processing the notification. For products imported into the UK the Competent Authority would be either the European Medicines Agency or the MHRA, depending on whether the product is centrally authorised or not.

UK legislation

The Human Medicines Regulations 2012 [SI 2012/1916] which came into force on 14 August 2012 modernises the UK's medicines legislation. It replaces most of the 1968 Medicines Act and over 200 statutory instruments, which had been cluttering up the statute book and complicating the law. This consolidated medicines legislation conjoins the statutory provisions for all licences, authorisations and registrations for medicines for human use.

Changes on the horizon

The new requirements introduced by the Falsified Medicines Directive for medicinal products to bear safety features (set out below) are to be the subject of a separate delegated act from the European Commission, and any standards for the use of them are still to be defined:

– the Qualified Person to ensure that they have been affixed.
– safey features not to be removed or covered unless the Manufacturing Authorisation Holder verifies that the medicinal product is authentic and has not been tampered with and that replacement safety features are equivalent and are applied in accordance with GMP.
– wholesale dealers to verify that any medicinal products they receive are not falsified, by checking that any "safety features" used on the outer packaging of a product are intact.
– brokers and wholesale dealers to record the batch numbers of, as a minimum, those products with safety features attached and for wholesale dealers to provide a record of batch numbers when supplying those products to their customers.

New guidelines at consultation, based on requirements in 2011/62/EU, on the principles of GDP for active substances for medicinal products for human use.

Rules and Guidance for Pharmaceutical Distributors 2014

This is the second edition of the "Rules & Guidance for Pharmaceutical Distributors". This is also the first edition issued by the MHRA as part of the new Medicines and Healthcare Products Regulatory Agency group. This new Rules and Guidance for Pharmaceutical Distributors 2014 brings together new and revised Commission written material concerning the distribution and brokering of medicines for human use and matters relating to the manufacture, importation and distribution of active substances.

Although it is UK legislation, implementing the Directives, that bears directly on activities in the UK, it is often helpful for wholesalers to be aware of the original EU obligations. This is particularly so when trading across boundaries of Member States. Therefore, the "Titles" or sections of Directive 2001/83/EC, as amended, dealing with the wholesale distribution of products for human use, brokering finished medicinal products and provisions relating to the manufacture, importation and distribution of active substances are included in this edition.

Revised sections to reflect the coming into force of the Human Medicines Regulations 2012 (SI 2012/1916) are provided. These Regulations consolidate the 1968 Medicines Act and its supporting regulations to set out a comprehensive regime for the authorisation of medicinal products for human use.

Other revised sections include:

- UK Guidance on Wholesale Distribution
- UK Legislation on Wholesale Distribution
- Glossary of Legislation

There are also new sections covering UK guidance and legislation for the brokering of finished medicinal products and the manufacture, importation and distribution of active substances.

Recommendations on meeting the important requirement to ensure the "proper conservation and distribution" of medicines requiring storage below ambient temperature ("cold-chain distribution") are reproduced here in updated form.

Updated sections on the activities and services of the Inspection, Enforcement and Standards Division of the MHRA, will be of interest to wholesalers. A new appendix has been added to provide the names of other human and veterinary medicines authorities in Europe.

Although much of the text in this book is available in its original form in other places, including various websites, we are pleased that "Rules and Guidance for Pharmaceutical Distributors 2014" continues to satisfy a demand for information in one authoritative and convenient place.

The 2014 version, will be available online, as part of "Medicines Complete" – a subscription-based database of leading medicines and healthcare references and for the first time it will be available in other E-reader formats. Going forward to keep up with changes to EU text and national provisions the print version of Rules and Guidance for Pharmaceutical Distributors 2014 will be revised and published annually. We hope that this new edition and the new formats will continue to be useful.

Gerald Heddell
Director, Inspection, Enforcement and Standards Division
September 2013

Acknowledgements

To the European Commission for permission to reproduce the text of the Directive and the EU guidelines on Good Distribution Practice.

To the Heads of Medicines Agencies for permission to reproduce the names and addresses of other human and veterinary medicines authorities in Europe.

Feedback

Comments on the content or presentation of the Orange Guide are encouraged and will be used to develop further editions. Your views are valued and both MHRA and Pharmaceutical Press would appreciate you taking the time to contact us. Please visit the feedback page at www.pharmpress.com/mhra-feedback or send your feedback to the address below:

"The Rules and Guidance for Pharmaceutical Distributors 2014"
Customer Services
Fourth Floor
MHRA
151 Buckingham Palace Road
Victoria
London SW1W 9SZ
UK
Tel.: +44 (0)20 3084 6000
Fax: +44 (0)20 3118 9803
E-mail: green.guide@mhra.gsi.gov.uk

Introduction

The distribution network for medicinal products has become increasingly complex and now involves many different players.

The obligation on governments of all Member States of the European Union and European Economic Area (EEA)[1] to ensure that pharmaceutical wholesale distributors are authorised is stated in Title VII of the Directive 2001/83/EC. This Title requires all authorised wholesale distributors to have available a Responsible Person (RP) and to comply with the Commission guidelines on Good Distribution Practice (GDP).

Title VII Directive 2001/83/EC has been amended as a result of the Falsified Medicines Directive 2011/62/EU and now requires brokers of medicines within the Community to be registered with their competent authority and to comply with appropriate GDP requirements. Amended Title IV of the Directive 2001/83/EC also requires importers, manufacturers and distributors of active substances who are established in the Union to register their activity with the competent authority of the Member State in which they are established.

The Commission guidelines for GDP first issued in 1993 has been revised as a consequence of the Falsified Medicines Directive to assist wholesale distributors in conducting their activities and to prevent falsified medicines from entering the legal supply chain. The revised guidelines also provides specific rules for persons involved in activities in relation to the sale or purchase of medicinal products whilst not conducting a wholesale activity i.e. brokers of medicines.

In the United Kingdom, the provisions for wholesale distributors, brokers of medicines and manufacturers, importers and distributors of active substances have been implemented by requirements and undertakings incorporated in the Human Medicines Regulations 2012 [SI 2012/1916]. Through these regulations compliance by wholesale distributors and brokers of medicines with the Commission guidelines of GDP is a statutory requirement.

---

[1] The member states of the European Community plus Iceland, Liechtenstein and Norway.

This publication brings together the new Commission guidelines on GDP, UK guidance on wholesale distribution practice and EU and UK legislation on wholesale distribution, which wholesale distributors are expected to follow when distributing medicinal products for human use. It is of particular relevance to authorised wholesale distributors and to their RPs, who have a responsibility for ensuring compliance with many of these regulatory requirements. Wholesale distributors are required to appoint an RP who has the knowledge and responsibility to ensure that correct procedures are followed during distribution. Updated notes on the qualifications and duties of RPs are included in this publication to assist this.

This publication is also of particular relevance to all brokers of medicines because it brings together UK guidance on brokering medicines and EU and UK legislation on brokering, which brokers are expected to follow when brokering medicinal products for human use.

It is also of relevance to importers and distributors of active substances. The manufacture of active substances for use in a licensed medicinal product must be in compliance with the relevant good manufacturing practice. These standards are currently described in Part II of the EU Commission Guidelines on Good Manufacturing Practice (GMP). Active substances imported from outside of the EEA must have been manufactured in accordance with standards of GMP at least equivalent to those in the EU. From the 2 July 2013 they must be accompanied by a written confirmation that equivalent GMP standards and supervision apply in the exporting country, unless the active substance is sourced from a country listed by the European Commission or exceptionally and where necessary to ensure availability of medicinal products an EU GMP certificate for the site of manufacture is available.

The European Commission will be adopting principles and guidelines for GMP for active substances, GDP guidelines for active substances and guidelines for the formal risk assessment process for excipients by means of delegated acts and guidelines.

This guide brings together UK guidance and EU and UK legislation on the importation and distribution of active substances, which importers and distributors of active substances are expected to follow when supplying active substances for use in licensed medicinal products for human use. For completeness this guide also includes matters on what manufacturers of active substances have to comply with in order to provide further background information for importers and distributors of active substances.

The aim of GMP and GDP is to assure the quality of the medicinal product for the safety, well-being and protection of the patient. In achieving this aim it is impossible to over-emphasise the importance of individuals, at all levels, in the assurance of the quality of medicinal products. This is emphasised in the first principle in the EC Guide to GMP. The great majority of reported defective medicinal products has resulted from human error or carelessness, not from failures in technology. All individuals involved with the distribution of medicinal products should bear this constantly in mind when performing their duties.

MHRA

MHRA: Licensing, Inspection and Enforcement for Human Medicines

Contents

Overview of the Medicines and Healthcare Products Regulatory Agency Group

In 2002, Ministers announced that the Medicines Control Agency and the Medical Devices Agency would be merged to form the Medicines and Healthcare products Regulatory Agency (MHRA). The MHRA is responsible for regulating all medicines and medical devices in the UK by ensuring they work and are acceptably safe.

On the 1 April 2013 the National Institute for Biological Standards and Control (NIBSC), previously part of the Health Protection Agency (HPA), became a new centre of the MHRA alongside the Clinical Practice Research Datalink (CPRD).

The MHRA and NIBSC have worked closely together for many years and have common interests in managing risks associated with biological medicines, facilitating development of new medicines safely and effectively, and maintaining UK expertise and ability to contribute to assuring the quality and safety of medicines in Europe and beyond.

These developments have created a new organisation that is a world leader in supporting science and research and the regulation of medicines and medical devices, strengthening the support provided to the UK's medicine's industry. The new Medicines and Healthcare Products Regulatory Agency group consists of:

- **MHRA Regulatory,** who protect health and improve lives by ensuring that medicines and medical devices work, and are acceptably safe; focusing on the core activities of product licensing, inspection and enforcement, and pharmacovigilance.
- **The Clinical Practice Research Datalink** (CPRD), which gives access to an unparalleled resource for conducting observational research and improving the efficiency of interventional research, across all areas of health, medicines and devices. CPRD joined the MHRA in 2012.
- **The National Institute for Biological Standards and Control,** world leaders in assuring the quality of biological medicines through product testing, developing standards and reference materials and carrying out applied research.

Medicines and Healthcare Products Regulatory Agency

MHRA	National Institute for Biological Standards Board (NIBSC)	Clinical Practice Research Datalink (CPRD)
• Operating a system of licensing, classification, monitoring (post-marketing surveillance) and enforcement for medicines. • Discharging statutory obligations for medical devices, including designating and monitoring the performance of notified bodies. • Ensuring statutory compliance in medicines clinical trials and assessing medical device clinical trials proposals. • Promulgating good practice in the safe use of medicines and medical devices. • Regulating the safety and quality of blood and blood components. • Discharging the functions of the UK Good Laboratory Practice Monitoring Authority (GLPMA). • Managing the activities of the British Pharmacopoeia (BP).	• Devising and drawing up standards for the purity and potency of biological substances and designing appropriate test procedures. • Preparing, approving, holding and distributing standard preparations of biological substances. • Providing, or arranging for, the provision of laboratory testing facilities for the testing of biological substances, carrying out such testing, examining records of manufacture and quality control and reporting on the results. • Carrying out or arranging for the carrying out of research in connection with biological standards and control functions.	• Managing and designing CPRD services to maximise the way anonymised NHS clinical data can be linked to enables many types of observational research and deliver research outputs that are beneficial to improving and safeguarding public health.

Overview of MHRA

All licensed medicines available in the UK are subject to rigorous scrutiny by the MHRA before they can be used by patients. This ensures that medicines meet acceptable standards on safety, quality and efficacy. It is the responsibility of the MHRA and the expert advisory bodies set up by the Human Medicines Regulations 2012 [SI 2012/1916] (previously under the 1968 Medicines Act) to ensure that the sometimes difficult balance between safety and effectiveness is achieved. MHRA experts assess all applications for new medicines to ensure they meet the required standards. This is followed up by a system of inspection and testing which continues throughout the lifetime of the medicine.

As the UK government's public health body which brings together the regulation of medicines and medical devices, science and research the roles of the MHRA are to:

- license medicines, manufacturers and distributors;
- register brokers of finished medicines and manufacturers, importers and distributors of active substances;
- regulate medical devices;
- approve UK clinical trials;
- monitor medicines and medical devices after licensing;
- ensure the safety and quality of blood;
- tackle illegal activity involving medicines, medical devices and blood;
- promote an understanding of the benefits and risks;
- facilitate the development of new medicines;
- support innovation in medicines and medical devices;
- be a leading provider of data and data services for healthcare research;
- work with international partners on issues;
- provide a national voice for the benefits and risks of medicines, medical devices and medical technologies.

The MHRA also hosts and supports a number of expert advisory bodies, including the Commission on Human Medicines (which replaced the Committee on the Safety of Medicines in 2005), and the British Pharmacopoeia Commission. In addition, as part of the European system of medicines approval, the MHRA or other national bodies may be the Rapporteur or Co-rapporteur for any given pharmaceutical application, taking on the bulk of the verification work on behalf of all members, while the documents are still sent to other members as and where requested.

Inspection, Enforcement and Standards Division

The MHRA's Inspection, Enforcement and Standards Division is responsible for ensuring compliance with the regulations and standards that apply to the manufacture, control and supply of medicines on the UK market.

Inspectorate

The Inspectorate Group in the MHRA's Inspection, Enforcement and Standards Division is comprised of dedicated units for Good Manufacturing Practice (GMP), Good Distribution Practice (GDP), Good Laboratory Practice (GLP), Good Clinical Practice (GCP) and Good Pharmacovigilance Practice (GPvP).

Good Manufacturing Practice (GMP)

GMP Inspectors conduct inspections of pharmaceutical manufacturers and other organisations to assess compliance with EC guidance on Good Manufacturing Practice and the relevant details contained in marketing authorisations and Clinical Trials Authorisations. They ensure that medicines supplied in the UK and wider EU meet consistent high standards of quality, safety and efficacy. Overseas manufacturing sites to be named on UK or EU marketing authorisations are also required to pass an inspection prior to approval of the marketing authorisation application. Following approval, a risk based inspection programme maintains on-going surveillance of UK and overseas manufacturing site compliance with EC GMP.

GMP Inspectors are responsible for inspecting and authorising a range of manufacturers of sterile and non-sterile dosage forms, biological products, investigational medicinal products, herbal products and active pharmaceutical ingredients, in addition to certain analytical laboratories. The manufacture of unlicensed medicines by holders of Manufacturer (Specials) Licences in the UK NHS and commercial sector is also inspected on a routine basis to assess compliance with relevant legislation and GMP.

The safety and quality of human blood for transfusion, or for further manufacture into blood-derived medicines, is ensured through inspections of relevant collection, processing, testing and storage activities at Blood Establishments and UK Hospital Blood Banks. These inspections assess compliance with specific UK and EU regulatory requirements, which take into account the detailed principles of GMP.

GMP Inspectors serve on a number of UK, EU and international technical and standards committees and provide help and advice to senior managers, Ministers and colleagues across the Agency, as necessary. Support and expertise is also provided to the inspection programmes of the European Medicines Agency (EMA), European Directorate for Quality of Medicines (EDQM), and the World Health Organization (WHO).

Good Distribution Practice (GDP)

GDP Inspectors conduct inspections of sites of wholesale dealers to assess compliance with EU Guidelines on Good Distribution Practice (GDP) and the conditions of a wholesale dealer's licence.

Inspectors will ensure that medicinal products are handled, stored and transported under conditions as prescribed by the marketing authorisation or product specification.

Inspections are undertaken of new applicants and then subsequently on a routine schedule based on a risk assessment of the site.

There are a number of developments that will impact on GDP during 2013 and going forward including:

- the Human Medicines Regulations 2012 [SI 2012/1916] which came into force in August 2012, replacing the majority of the Medicines Act 1968 and its supporting legislation;
- the transposition of the Falsified Medicines Directive 2011/62/EU into UK medicines legislation which extends GDP to any person or entity who procures, stores or supplies medicinal products, for export to countries outside of the European Economic Area (EEA) and to brokers of finished medicines within the EEA.
- the application of the revised EU Guidelines on GDP which entered into force on 8 September 2013. The revised guidelines introduce the following changes:
  - the maintenance of a quality system setting out responsibilities, processes and risk management principles in relation to wholesale activities;
  - suitable documentation which prevents errors from spoken communication;
  - sufficient competent personnel to carry out all the tasks for which the wholesale distributor is responsible;
  - adequate premises, installations and equipment so as to ensure proper storage and distribution of medicinal products;
  - appropriate management of complaints, returns, suspected falsified medicinal products and recalls;
  - outsourced activities correctly defined to avoid misunderstandings;
  - rules for transport in particular to protect medicinal products against breakage, adulteration and theft, and to ensure that temperature conditions are maintained within acceptable limits during transport;
  - specific rules for brokers (person involved in activities in relation to the sale or purchase of medicinal products, except for wholesale distribution, that do not include physical handling the products).

The revised EU Guidelines on GDP have been included in this publication.

Good Laboratory Practice (GLP)

GLP Inspectors conduct inspections of UK facilities that carry out non-clinical studies for submission to domestic and international regulatory authorities to assess the safety of new chemicals to humans, animals and the environment. These inspections are designed to assure that studies are performed in accordance with the relevant EC directives and the Organisation for Economic Co-operation and Development (OECD) principles as required by OECD Council acts relating to the Mutual Acceptance of Data. The range of test facilities to be monitored include those involved in the testing of human and veterinary pharmaceuticals, agrochemicals, food and feed additives, industrial chemicals and cosmetics.

Good Clinical Practice (GCP)

The GCP Inspectorate is responsible for inspecting clinical trials for compliance with Good Clinical Practice. Compliance with this good practice provides assurance that the rights, safety and well-being of trial subjects are protected, and that the results of the clinical trials are credible and accurate.

The function of the GCP Inspectorate is to assess the compliance of organisations with UK and EU legislation relating to the conduct of clinical trials in investigational medicinal products. This is achieved through carrying out inspections of sponsor organisations that hold Clinical Trial Authorisations (CTA), organisations that provide services to clinical trial sponsors or investigator sites.

Good Pharmacovigilance Practice (GPvP)

The Pharmacovigilance Inspectorate conducts inspections of the pharmacovigilance systems of marketing authorisation holders to assess compliance with the requirements of the UK and European legislation and guidelines relating to the monitoring of the safety of medicines given to patients.

The Data Processing Group

The Data Processing Group was formed in 2011 by consolidating the existing Process Licensing, Export Certificates, Import Notifications and Defective Medicines Reporting Centre functions to reside in a single Business Unit as part of the Inspection, Enforcement and Standards Division.

Manufacturer's and Wholesale Dealer's Licence/Authorisations

Manufacture of and wholesale dealing in medicinal products are licensable activities under UK and EU legislation. These licences are referred to as process licences and include a wide range of licences covering diverse activities listed below:

- Licences for the manufacture/importation of licensed medicinal products for human use, commonly abbreviated to MIA.
- "Specials" licences for the manufacture/importation of unlicensed medicinal products for human use, commonly abbreviated to MS.
- Authorisations for the manufacture/importation of Investigational Medicinal Products for human use, commonly abbreviated to MIA (IMP).
- Authorisations for the manufacture/importation of licensed medicinal products for veterinary use, commonly abbreviated to ManA.
- "Specials" licences for the manufacture of unlicensed medicinal products for veterinary use, commonly abbreviated to ManSA.
- Authorisation for the manufacture of Exempt Advanced Therapy Medicinal Products, commonly abbreviated to MeAT.
- Licences for the wholesale dealing of medicinal products for human use, commonly abbreviated to WL and/or WDL (including those covering unlicensed medicines obtained from another EEA Member State).
- Licences for the wholesale dealing/importation of medicinal products for veterinary use, commonly abbreviated to WDA.
- Blood Establishment Authorisations, commonly abbreviated to BEA.

The Data Processing team process all applications for new licences, variations to existing licences, changes of ownership, terminations, cancellations as well as suspensions and revocations on the Inspection Action Group's instruction, making extensive use of computer technology to do so. They are also responsible for issuing Certificates of Good Manufacturing Practice (GMP) and Good Distribution Practice (GDP) on behalf of the GMP and GDP Inspectorate.

Registrations

The Falsified Medicines Directive 2011/62/EU made it a requirement that certain activities require registration and that a minimum of information be published on a publically accessible registers. These activities include:

- Brokering of finished human medicines.
- Manufacture, importation and distribution of active substances.

The Data Processing team process all applications for registration, variations to existing registrations, annual compliance reports, terminations, cancellations, suspensions and revocations making extensive use of computer technology to do so.

Export Certificates

The Data Processing team are also responsible for issuing certificates in support of the World Health Organization (WHO) scheme on the quality of pharmaceutical products moving in international commerce (often referred to as export certificates):

- Certificate of a pharmaceutical product (CPP). This certificate complies with the WHO format.
- Certificate of licensing status (CLS). This certificate complies with the WHO format.
- Certificate of manufacturing status (CMS).
- Certificate for the importation of a pharmaceutical constituent (CPC).
- Statement of licensing status of a pharmaceutical product(s).

Importing Unlicensed Medicines – Import Notifications

Under regulation 46 of the Human Medicines Regulations 2012 [SI 2012/1916] a medicine, must have a marketing authorisation ("Product Licence") unless exempt. One of these exemptions, which is in regulation 167 to these regulations, is for the importation and supply of unlicensed medicinal products for the special needs of individual patients, commonly, but incorrectly called "named patients". Prospective importers must hold a relevant licence and must notify the MHRA of their intention to import:

- for import from within the European Economic Area (EEA), a Wholesale Dealer's Licence valid for import and handling unlicensed relevant medicinal products;
- for import from outside of the EEA, a Manufacturer's 'Specials' Licence valid for import.

The Data Processing team makes use of a bespoke computer system (INS) to enter the information, refer flagged requests to Pharmaceutical Assessors for assessment as required and issue confirmation letters authorising or rejecting importation.

Defective Medicines Report Centre (DMRC)

The MHRA's Defective Medicines Report Centre (DMRC) plays a major part in the protection of public health by minimising the hazard to patients arising from the distribution of defective medicinal products. It does this by providing an emergency assessment and communications system between suppliers of medicinal products, the regulatory authorities and the users. It achieves this by receiving and assessing reports of suspected defective medicines, monitoring and as necessary advising and directing appropriate actions by the responsible authorisation holder and communicating the details of this action as necessary and with appropriate urgency to recipients of the products and other interested parties in the UK and elsewhere by means of drug alerts.

Manufacturers and importers are obliged to report to the licensing authority (MHRA) any quality defect in a medicinal product which could result in a recall or restriction on supply. Other users and distributors of medicinal products are encouraged to do this.

Where a defective medicine is considered to present a risk to public health, the marketing authorisation holder, or the manufacturer as appropriate, is responsible for recalling the affected batch(es) or, in extreme cases, removing all batches of the product from the market. The DMRC will normally support this action by the issue of a drug alert notification to healthcare professionals. Drug alerts are classed from 1 to 4 according to their criticality and the speed with which action must be taken to remove the defective medicine from the distribution chain and, where necessary, from the point of dispensing and use. This varies from immediate action for a Class 1 alert, to action within five days for a Class 3 alert. In some low-risk circumstances the product may be allowed to remain in the supply chain when the DMRC will issue a Class 4 "caution in use" alert.

The DMRC is also part of the European Rapid Alert System, and in the case of Class 1 and Class 2 will notify regulators in other countries using the European Rapid Alert System.

Enforcement Group

Medicines legislation contains statutory provisions to enforce the requirements of the Human Medicines Regulations 2012 [SI 2012/1916] and the remaining provisions of the 1968 Medicines Act.

This enforcement role is carried out by the MHRA's Enforcement Group which is comprised of a Case Referrals Team, Intelligence Analysts, Investigations Team, Prosecution Unit and Policy/Relationships management.

The legislation confers certain powers, including rights of entry, powers of inspection, seizure, sampling and production of documents. Duly authorised Investigation Officers investigate cases using these powers and, where appropriate, criminal prosecutions are brought by the Crown Prosecution Service (CPS). MHRA investigators also investigate offences under other legislation such as the Fraud Act, Trademarks Act and the Offences Against the Person Act.

All reported breaches of medicines legislation are investigated. Reports are processed and risk-assessed before a course of action is agreed in line with our published Enforcement Strategy.

The aim of the Intelligence Unit is to drive forward the implementation of intelligence-led enforcement and enable a more proactive approach to the acquisition and development of information. The Unit acts as a co-ordination point for all information-gathering activities and works in conjunction with a wide network of public and professional bodies and trade associations, e.g. UK Border Force, UK Border Agency, Department of Health, Trading Standards and Port Health Authorities, the Police Service; and professional organisations such as the General Pharmaceutical Council (GPhC), General Medical Council and the Association of the British Pharmaceutical Industry (ABPI). Additionally, there is a network of other regulatory agencies and law enforcement bodies within the European Community and in other countries through which the Enforcement Group can exchange information and follow trends in pharmaceutical crime.

The Enforcement Group monitors trends in pharmaceutical crime and co-ordinates initiatives to counteract criminal activity. In particular, the availability of counterfeit medicines is a key priority area and an anti-counterfeiting strategy has been agreed and implemented.

Advice

The MHRA publishes a series of Guidance Notes relating to its statutory functions. Those of particular interest to manufacturers and wholesale dealers include:

GN 5   Notes for applicants and holders of a manufacturer's licence
GN 6   Notes for applicants and holders of a wholesale dealer's licence
GN 8   A guide to what is a medicinal product
GN 14 Supply of unlicensed medicinal products "Specials".

These Guidance Notes and a list of others available may be obtained from the MHRA's website or from the MHRA's Customer Services Team.

Contact details are as follows:

Address:
Customer Services, MHRA,
151 Buckingham Palace Road, Victoria, London SW1W 9SZ, UK
Telephone: +44 (0)20 3084 6000 (weekdays 0900–1700)
Fax: +44 (0)20 3118 9803
E-mail: info@mhra.gsi.gov.uk
Website: www.mhra.gov.uk

2

UK Guidance on the Manufacture, Importation and Distribution of Active Substances

Contents

Introduction

EU Directive 2001/83/EC lays down the rules for the manufacture, import, marketing and supply of medicinal products and ensures the functioning of the internal market for medicinal products while safeguarding a high level of protection of public health in the EU.

The falsification of medicinal products is a global problem, requiring effective and enhanced international coordination and cooperation in order to ensure that anti-falsification strategies are more effective, in particular as regards sale of such products via the Internet. To that end, the Commission and Member States are cooperating closely and supporting ongoing work in international fora on this subject, such as the Council of Europe, Europol and the United Nations. In addition, the Commission, working closely with Member States, is cooperating with the competent authorities of third countries with a view to effectively combating the trade in falsified medicinal products at a global level.

Active substances are those substances which give a medicinal product its therapeutic effect. They are the Active Pharmaceutical Ingredient (API).

Falsified active substances and active substances that do not comply with applicable requirements of Directive 2001/83/EC pose serious risks to public health.

The Falsified Medicines Directive 2011/62/EU amends Directive 2001/83/EC in order to facilitate the enforcement of and control of compliance with Union rules relating to active substances. It makes a number of significant changes to the controls on active substances intended for use in the manufacture of a medicinal product for human use.

A number of new terms have been introduced into the 2001 Directive by the Falsified Medicines Directive, including "falsified medicinal product" and "active substance". The aim of this is to ensure that other amendments introduced by the Falsified Medicines Directive are consistently interpreted and applied across the European Union.

The 2001 Directive has been amended to permit the European Commission to adopt the following:

- the principles and guidelines of good manufacturing practice for active substances, by means of a delegated act;
- the principles of good distribution practice for active substances, by means of adopted guidelines.

Registration

To provide a greater level of control, and transparency of supply, for active substances within the European Community manufacturers, importers and distributors of active substances have to notify the relevant National Competent Authorities of their activities and provide certain details. In the UK this will be the MHRA. The National Competent Authority has an obligation to enter these details into a Community Database following the determination of a successful application for registration. The National Competent Authority may then conduct inspections against the requirements of the relevant good practices before permitting such businesses to start trading. Manufacturers, importers and distributors of active substances will not only be subject to inspection on the basis of suspicions of non-compliance, but also on the basis of risk-analysis.

Authorised manufacturers of medicinal products who also manufacture and/or import active substances, either for use in their own products or products manufactured by other companies, are not exempt from the requirement to register.

Persons who are requested to import an active substance from a non-EEA country that provide facilities solely for transporting the active substance, or where they are acting as an import agent, imports the active substance solely to the order of another person who holds a certificate of good manufacturing practice issued by the licensing authority, are not required to register.

The registration regime for manufacturers, importers and distributors of active substances will be subject to an application procedure, followed by a determination procedure completed by the MHRA.

The person applying for registration must notify the MHRA immediately of any changes which have taken place as regards to the information in the registration form, where such changes may have an impact on quality or safety of the active substances that are manufactured, imported or distributed. These changes shall be treated as incorporated in the application form.

The MHRA must grant or refuse an application for registration within 60 working days beginning immediately after the day on which a valid application is received.

The MHRA will notify the applicant within 60 days of receipt of a valid application for registration whether they intend to undertake an inspection.

The applicant may not undertake any activity before either:

- 60 days have elapsed and the applicant has not been notified of the Agency's intention to inspect, or
- following inspection the Agency has notified the applicant that they may commence their activities.

After inspection the MHRA will prepare a report and communicate that report to the applicant. The applicant will have the opportunity to respond to the report. Within 90 days of an inspection the MHRA shall issue an appropriate good practice certificate to the applicant, indicating that the applicant complies with the requirements of the relevant good practices. Where an applicant is found to be non-compliant with the requisite standards, a statement of non-compliance will be issued by the MHRA.

If after 60 days of the receipt of the application form the MHRA has not notified the applicant of their intention to carry out an inspection, the applicant may commence their business activity and regard themselves as registered. The MHRA will issue a certificate to the applicant and enter the details into the Community Database.

This Community Database which is publicly available will enable National Competent Authorities in other EEA Member States or other legal entities, to establish the bona fides and compliance of manufacturers, importers and distributors of active substances established in the UK and those in other EEA territories. The MHRA will investigate concerns with regards to UK registrations of non-compliance and reciprocal arrangements will apply with other EEA Member States.

Conditions of Registration as a Manufacturer, Importer or Distributor of an Active Substance

A person in the UK may not import, manufacture or distribute, an active substance for use in a licensed human medicine unless they are registered with the MHRA in accordance with the Human Medicines Regulations 2012 and the respective conditions of those Regulations are met.

Registration holders must submit to the MHRA an annual update of any changes to the information provided in the application. Any changes which may have an impact on the quality or safety of the active substance which the registrant is permitted to handle must be notified to the Agency immediately.

An annual compliance report will need to be submitted:

- in relation to any application made before 31 March 2013, the date of application; and
- in relation to each subsequent reporting year, 30 April following the end of that year.

Where the Commission has adopted principles and guidelines of good manufacturing practice under the third paragraph of Article 47[1] of the 2001 Directive which applies to an active substance manufactured in the UK, the registered manufacturer must comply with good manufacturing practice in relation to that active substance.

Where the Commission has adopted principles and guidelines of good distribution practice under the fourth paragraph of Article 47 of the 2001 Directive which applies to an active substance distributed in the United Kingdom, the registered distributor must comply with good distribution practice in relation to that active substance.

Where the Commission has adopted principles and guidelines of good manufacturing practice under the third paragraph of Article 47 of the 2001 Directive which applies to an active substance imported into the UK and where an active substance is imported from a third country the registered importer must comply with good distribution practice in relation to the active substance.

Under such circumstances the active substances must have been manufactured in accordance with standards which are at least equivalent to EU good manufacturing practice and when imported must be accompanied by a written confirmation from the competent authority of the exporting third country unless a waiver exists.

---

[1] Article 47 was amended by Directive 2011/62/EU of the European Parliament and of the Council (OJ No L 174, 1.7.2011, p. 74).

GMP for Active Substances

Directive 2001/83/EC has been amended to include a new definition of "active substance" which means any substance or mixture of substances intended to be used in the manufacture of a medicinal product and that, when used in its production, becomes an active ingredient of that product intended to exert a pharmacological, immunological or metabolic action with a view to restoring, correcting or modifying physiological functions or to make a medical diagnosis.

The manufacture of active substances should be subject to good manufacturing practice regardless of whether those active substances are manufactured in the Union or imported. Where active substances are manufactured in third countries it should be ensured that such substances have been manufactured to the relevant European standards of good manufacturing practice (GMP), so as to provide a level of protection of public health equivalent to that provided for by EU law.

A manufacturer or assembler of an active substance will have to comply with the principles and guidelines for GMP for active substances. Manufacture, in relation to an active substance, includes any process carried out in the course of making the substance and the various processes of dividing up, packaging, and presentation of the active substance. Assemble, in relation to an active substance, includes the various processes of dividing up, packaging and presentation of the substance, and "assembly" has a corresponding meaning. These activities will be the subject of a GMP certificate.

Importers of an active substance from a third country have to comply with the guidelines for Good Distribution Practice (GDP) in relation to the active substance. This activity will be the subject of a GDP certificate.

Distributors of an active substance within the UK which has been sourced from a manufacturer or an importer within the EU will have to comply with the guidelines for GDP for active substances. This activity will be the subject of a GDP certificate.

The 2001 Directive has been amended to permit the European Commission to adopt the following:

- the principles and guidelines of good manufacturing practice for active substances, by means of a delegated act; and
- the principles of good distribution practice for active substances, by means of adopted guidelines.

GMP for active substances is contained in Part II of the EU guidelines on Good Manufacturing Practice.

GDP for Active Substances

In February 2013 the European Commission consulted on its draft "Guidelines on the principles of good distribution practices for active substances for medicinal products for human use".

The draft text sets out the quality system elements for the procuring, importing, holding, supplying or exporting active substances. However the scope of the proposed text excludes activities consisting of re-packaging, re-labelling or dividing up of active substances which are manufacturing activities and as such are subject to the guidelines on Good Manufacturing Practice of active substances. The draft text of the guidelines covers:

- Quality System
- Personnel
- Documentation
- Orders
- Procedures
- Records
- Premises and Equipment
- Receipt
- Storage
- Deliveries to Customers
- Transfer of Information
- Returns
- Complaints and Recalls
- Self-inspections.

Written Confirmation

The Falsified Medicines Directive modifies EU Medicines Directive 2001/83/EC and from 2 July 2013 introduces new requirements for active substances imported into the European Economic Area (EEA) for use in the manufacture of authorised medicinal products.

The Falsified Medicines Directive requires importers of active substances to obtain written confirmations from competent authorities in non-EEA countries ("third countries") that the standards of manufacture of active substances at manufacturing sites on their territory are equivalent to EU good manufacturing practice (EU GMP). These confirmations are required before importation of active substances into the EU.

Each shipment of active substance received should be accompanied by a written confirmation from the Competent Authority of the exporting third country, stating that the active substance has been:

- manufactured to GMP standards at least equivalent to those laid down in the European Union;
- the third country manufacturing plant is subject to regular, strict and transparent inspections, and effective enforcement of GMP;
- in the event of non-conformance of the manufacturing site on inspection, such findings will be communicated to the European Union without delay.

The template for the written confirmation has been published in Part III of EudraLex, Volume 4 and is included in Chapter 2 of the Orange Guide.

Waiver from Written Confirmation

The Falsified Medicines Directive provides two waivers if written confirmations are not provided. The first is where the regulatory framework applicable to active substances in those third countries has been assessed by the European Commission (EC) as providing an equivalent level of protection of public health over active substance manufacture and distribution to those applied in the EU. This assessment follows a request from the exporting third country's Competent Authority, and considers the regulatory framework for active substance manufacture and control and its equivalence to EU standards. Only if the exporting country is on the EC's ("white") list is the requirement for a written confirmation from that country's Competent Authority removed.

The second waiver is where the third country active substance manufacturing site has been inspected by an EU member state, has issued a certificate of compliance with EU-GMP and that it remains within its period of validity. This is an exceptional waiver intended to apply where it is necessary to ensure the availability of medicinal products. Member States using this waiver should communicate this fact to the European Commission in accordance with the legislation (Article 46b(4)). MHRA has notified the European Commission of its intent to use this waiver should that be necessary.

Procedure for Active Substance Importation

A summary of the overall active substance import process has been developed to promote a common expectation and common approaches by Member States and is available on the Heads of Medicines Agencies, website: http://www.hma.eu/43.html. The flow chart is reproduced here:

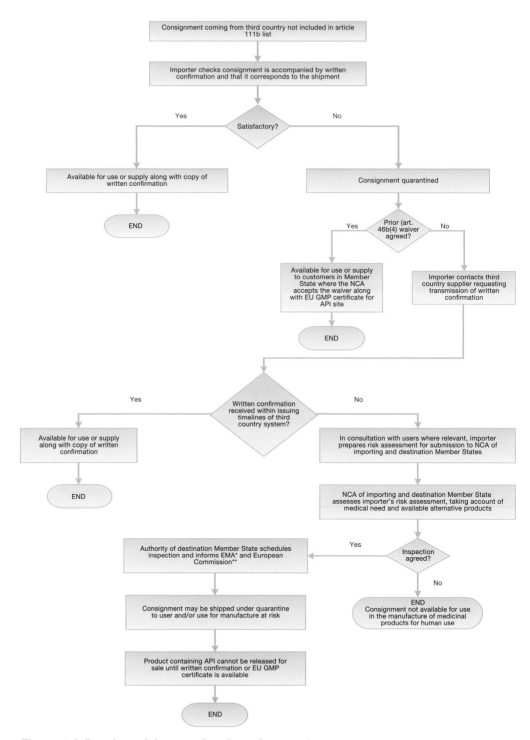

Figure 1 A flowchart of the overall active substance import process
*GMPINS@ema.europa.eu
**sanco-pharmaceuticals-d6@ec.europa.eu

Procedure for Waiver from Written Confirmation

UK based companies (registered importers and manufacturers who also import directly) who wish to import active substances under the second waiver should apply to gmpinspectorate@mhra.gsi.gov.uk using the form provided below which is available on the MHRA website.

Application Form for a waiver from the requirement to supply Written Confirmation with consignments of an imported Active Substance on the basis of a GMP certification of the Active Substance Manufacturer by an EEA Member State

A. Details of Third Country Manufacturing Site
Name of Active Substance   :_____
(Note: Only one active substance permitted per Waiver application. Use INN nomenclature)

Name of Active Substance Manufacturer   :_____
Address of Active Substance Manufacturer   :_____
_____
_____
                        Country   :_____
Third Country Competent Authority   :_____
site / facility reference number (if known)

B. Reason for Application for this Waiver
The manufacturer / importer should attach a document explaining the reason for requesting this waiver. It should be noted that if the active substance is being sourced from a third country where the authority there is known to issue Written Confirmations then under normal circumstances it would be expected that a Written Confirmation would be the basis for importation of active substances from that country.

C. Details of GMP Certification
Any differences between the name and address supplied above and those details supplied on the GMP certificate must be justified in order to ensure efficient processing of the application.
Name of authority which issued the GMP certificate   :_____
Inspection Date Referenced on GMP certificate   :_____
Period of validity of GMP certificate* (if stated)   :_____
(*this is 3 years unless there is a statement to the contrary)
Please attach a copy of the GMP certificate to this application form.

D. Details of Waiver Applicant
The Waiver Application may be submitted either by a site which has been registered with the MHRA for importation activities in the UK relating to active substances or by an authorised manufacturer / importer of human medicines in the UK which is using the imported active substance for manufacture of medicines for human use (excludes Investigational Medicinal Products) at its manufacturing address. If the importation activities (purchase of the active substance from a third country site or acting as the direct site of physical importation of the active substance) are being carried out directly by an authorised manufacturer of human medicines then both sections D1 and D2 below should be completed.

D1. Active Substance Importer
Active Substance Importers Registration No.:_____
Importation activity carried out for this active substance
(tick all that apply)   ☐ Procurement (Purchasing)   ☐ Site of physical importation
Registered Name of Importer :_____

Registered Address of Importer :_____

_____

_____

Country   UK

D2. Authorised Manufacturer of Human Medicines using Imported Active Substance
Manufacturer's / Importers Authorisation No. : _____
Name of Authorised Manufacturer   : _____
Manufacturing Site Address   : _____

_____

_____

Country   UK

E. Signature of Waiver Applicant
Signature   :_____ Date:_____
Name (Print) :_____
Position   :_____

F. Decision by MHRA on Waiver
Waiver Number:_____
Waiver approved (Yes / No):_____
Signature:_____ Date:_____
Name (Print):_____
Position :_____

National Contingency Guidance

The MHRA acknowledges that the introduction of these additional requirements may in some instance make the sourcing of active substances from some third countries difficult in the short term following 2 July 2013. The MHRA has therefore developed contingency plans that would allow the Agency, in cases where there is an overriding need to ensure continued supply of specific active substances after 2 July 2013, to provide an opinion on the importation of the active substance to permit manufacture, QP certification and supply of finished medicinal products. The aim of these contingency plans is to ensure, as per the aims of the Falsified Medicines Directive, the continued supply of active substances of appropriate quality and maintain the responsibility for the quality of the authorised medicinal products with the manufacturer, as is the case under the current legislation in force. Where these supply difficulties exist, please contact the GMP inspectorate at GMPinspectorate@mhra.gsi.gov.uk.

Therefore for the short term only and where:

(a) the third country active substance manufacturing site is not covered by a written confirmation; and

(b) the exporting country has not been assessed by the EC as having standards equivalent to EU GMP; and

(c) the third country active substance manufacturing site is not the subject, following inspection, of a current certificate of compliance with EU GMP,

the MHRA is actively seeking further information from impacted UK manufacturing sites identified through the active substance mapping exercise. Where UK Manufacturing Authorisation Holders ("MIA Holder") have determined that their third country active substance sources are at risk and have not been contacted by MHRA they should provide evidence in a submission / declaration template that:

(a) the active substance manufacturing site has been audited in the last three years either by himself or by a third party acting on his behalf and found to be operating in compliance with EU GMP for active substances; and

(b) the third country active substance manufacturing site is the subject, following inspection, of a current certificate of compliance with GMP issued by a recognised national authority or international organisation e.g. US-FDA, EU-MRA partners, EU-ACCA partners, PIC/S member states and the WHO.

UK based companies (registered importers and manufacturers who also import directly) who wish to import active substances under this guidance should apply to GMPinspectorate@mhra.gsi.gov.uk using the form provided at the end of this section which is available on the MHRA website.

Where the MIA Holder can make the first declaration but cannot declare that the third country active substance manufacturing site is the subject, following inspection, of a current certificate of compliance with GMP issued by a recognised national authority or international organisation then the MHRA intends to enter details of the third country active substance manufacturing site onto a database of pending GMP inspection of a third country active substance manufacturing site.

The MHRA will conduct further assessment of the data supplied in the submission(s) at the next routine reinspection of these finished product manufacturing sites.

The entry on the database will be removed if the active substance manufacturing site and the AS subsequently become the subject of a written confirmation, the third country has been assessed as having standards equivalent to GMP, or the AS manufacturing site, following inspection has been issued with a certificate of compliance with EU GMP. The pending-inspection database will only be available as long as this is required as a contingency measure.

Importers of active substances are also asked to note that where the sourcing of active substances from some third countries is difficult because it is not covered by a written confirmation, the exporting country has not been assessed as equivalent and the active substance manufacturing site is not the subject of a valid GMP certificate, these circumstances are subject to on-going review coordinated at an EU level. A key element of this review is the gathering of further data from EU-based finished product manufacturers for active substance import risk assessment and, where required, the EU level coordination of third country active substance manufacturer inspections.

National Contingency Guidance Submission Template

PART A: Finished Product Manufacturer to which this declaration applies

Name and address of MIA holder	Authorisation number

PART B: Concerned Third Country Active Substance Manufacturing Site

Name and Address of Active Substance Manufacturing Site
Name of Active Substances manufactured at this site

PART C: Basis of declaration in lieu of full compliance with Article 46b(2)

Please tick to confirm that an on-site audit of the active substance manufacturer has been conducted by the MIA holder or by a third party on their behalf

(i)   ☐   On-site audit of the active substance manufacturer(s) conducted by MIA holder or by a third party on their behalf:

An on site audit of the active substance(s) manufactured at the site listed in PART B has been completed either by the MIAH(s) listed below or by a third party auditing body i.e. contract acceptor(s) on behalf of the MIAH i.e. contract giver(s) as listed:

MIAH (or contract giver)	Auditing body (contract acceptor)	Site audited	Date of audit[1]

[1]The date of the last audit should not exceed 3 years.

(ii)   Availability of a current[2] certificate of compliance with GMP issued by a recognised national authority or international organisation e.g. EDQM-CEP, US-FDA, EU-MRA partners, EU-ACCA partners, PIC/S member states and the WHO.

  ☐   A current certificate for the site named in Section B of compliance with GMP issued by a recognised national authority or international organisation **is** available.
  ☐   A current certificate for the site named in Section B of compliance with GMP issued by a recognised national authority or international organisation **is not** available.

Inspection Authority	Date of inspection

[2]The date of the last inspection should not exceed 3 years.

(iii) **Supplementary supportive information (optional):**

For the active substance manufacturing site listed, results of inspection report(s) or GMP certificate(s) issued by recognised national authorities or international organisations together with other supporting information are attached.

Summary of supporting information provided

PART D: Declaration

I declare that:
QP Responsibility

- I am a QP with specific responsibility for GMP compliance of the active substance manufactured at the sites listed in Part B and am authorised to make this declaration.
- That the audit report(s) and all the other documentation relating to this declaration of GMP compliance of the active substance manufacturer(s) will be made available for inspection by the competent authorities, if requested.

GMP Compliance

- The manufacture of the named active substance(s) at the site given in Part B is in accordance with the detailed guideline on good manufacturing practice for active substances used as starting materials as required by Article 46(f) of Directive 2001/83/EC as amended.
- This is based upon an on-site audit of the active substance manufacturer.
- That the outcome of the audit confirms that the active substance manufacturer complies with the principles and guidelines of good manufacturing practice.

Audit

- In the case of third party audit(s), I have evaluated each of the named contract acceptor(s) give in Part C and that technical contractual arrangements are in place and that any measures taken by the contract giver(s) are documented e.g. signed undertakings by the auditor(s).
- In all cases, the audit(s) was/were conducted by properly qualified and trained staff, in accordance with approved procedures.

Inspection, of the third country AS manufacturing site by a recognised national authority or international organisation

- Where available results of inspection report(s) or GMP certificate(s) issued by recognised national authorities or international organisations are within their period of validity and are attached together with other supporting information.

Part E: Name and Signature of QP responsible for this Declaration

This declaration is submitted by:

Status (job title)

Signatory _____ _____

MIAH name:

Print name _____ _____

MIAH number:

Date _____ _____

Legislation on Manufacture and Importation

3

EU Legislation on Manufacture and Importation

Contents

DIRECTIVE 2001/83/EC, TITLE IV, MANUFACTURE AND IMPORTATION

Directive 2001/83/EC of the European Parliament and of the Council of 6 November 2001 on the Community code relating to medicinal products for human use

Title IV: Manufacture and Importation

> Editor's note   Articles 46a, 46b, 47, 52a and 52b of Title IV of this directive is reproduced below. Reference should be made to the full Directive for the preamble, definitions and the general and final provisions.

Article 46a

1   For the purposes of this Directive, manufacture of active substances used as starting materials shall include both total and partial manufacture or import of an active substance used as a starting material as defined in Part I, point 3.2.1.1 (b) Annex I, and the various processes of dividing up, packaging or presentation prior to its incorporation into a medicinal product, including repackaging or relabelling, such as are carried out by a distributor of starting materials.

2   The Commission shall be empowered to adapt paragraph 1 to take account of scientific and technical progress. That measure, designed to amend non-essential elements of this Directive, shall be adopted in accordance with the regulatory procedure with scrutiny referred to in Article 121(2a).

Article 46b

1   Member States shall take appropriate measures to ensure that the manufacture, import and distribution on their territory of active substances, including active substances that are intended for export, comply with good manufacturing practice and good distribution practices for active substances.

2   Active substances shall only be imported if the following conditions are fulfilled:

(a) the active substances have been manufactured in accordance with standards of good manufacturing practice at least equivalent to those laid down by the Union pursuant to the third paragraph of Article 47; and

(b) the active substances are accompanied by a written confirmation from the competent authority of the exporting third country of the following:

   (i) the standards of good manufacturing practice applicable to the plant manufacturing the exported active substance are at least equivalent to those laid down by the Union pursuant to the third paragraph of Article 47;

   (ii) the manufacturing plant concerned is subject to regular, strict and transparent controls and to the effective enforcement of good manufacturing practice, including repeated and unannounced inspections, so as to ensure a protection of public health at least equivalent to that in the Union; and

   (iii) in the event of findings relating to non- compliance, information on such findings is supplied by the exporting third country to the Union without any delay.

This written confirmation shall be without prejudice to the obligations set out in Article 8 and in point (f) of Article 46.

3 The requirement set out in point (b) of paragraph 2 of this Article shall not apply if the exporting country is included in the list referred to in Article 111b.

4 Exceptionally and where necessary to ensure the availability of medicinal products, when a plant manufacturing an active substance for export has been inspected by a Member State and was found to comply with the principles and guidelines of good manufacturing practice laid down pursuant to the third paragraph of Article 47, the requirement set out in point (b) of paragraph 2 of this Article may be waived by any Member State for a period not exceeding the validity of the certificate of Good Manufacturing Practice. Member States that make use of the possibility of such waiver, shall communicate this to the Commission.

Article 47

The principles and guidelines of good manufacturing practices for medicinal products referred to in Article 46(f) shall be adopted in the form of a directive. That measure, designed to amend non-essential elements of this Directive by supplementing it, shall be adopted in accordance with the regulatory procedure with scrutiny referred to in Article 121(2a).

Detailed guidelines in line with those principles will be published by the Commission and revised necessary to take account of technical and scientific progress.

The Commission shall adopt, by means of delegated acts in accordance with Article 121a and subject to the conditions laid down in Articles 121b and 121c, the principles and guidelines of good manufacturing practice for active substances referred to in the first paragraph of point (f) of Article 46 and in Article 46b.

The principles of good distribution practices for active substances referred to in the first paragraph of point (f) of Article 46 shall be adopted by the Commission in the form of guidelines.

The Commission shall adopt guidelines on the formalised risk assessment for ascertaining the appropriate good manufacturing practice for excipients referred to in the second paragraph of point (f) of Article 46.

Article 52a

1   Importers, manufacturers and distributors of active substances who are established in the Union shall register their activity with the competent authority of the Member State in which they are established.

2   The registration form shall include, at least, the following information:

(i)   name or corporate name and permanent address;

(ii)   the active substances which are to be imported, manufactured or distributed;

(iii) particulars regarding the premises and the technical equipment for their activity.

3   The persons referred to in paragraph 1 shall submit the registration form to the competent authority at least 60 days prior to the intended commencement of their activity.

4   The competent authority may, based on a risk assessment, decide to carry out an inspection. If the competent authority notifies the applicant within 60 days of the receipt of the registration form that an inspection will be carried out, the activity shall not begin before the competent authority has notified the applicant that he may commence the activity. If within 60 days of the receipt of the registration form the competent authority has not notified the applicant that an inspection will be carried out, the applicant may commence the activity.

5   The persons referred to in paragraph 1 shall communicate annually to the competent authority an inventory of the changes which have taken place as regards the information provided in the registration form. Any changes that may have an impact on the quality or safety of the active substances

that are manufactured, imported or distributed must be notified immediately.

6   Persons referred to in paragraph 1 who had commenced their activity before 2 January 2013 shall submit the registration form to the competent authority by 2 March 2013.

7   Member States shall enter the information provided in accordance with paragraph 2 of this Article in the Union database referred to in Article 111(6).

8   This Article shall be without prejudice to Article 111.

Article 52b

1   Notwithstanding Article 2(1), and without prejudice to Title VII, Member States shall take the necessary measures in order to prevent medicinal products that are introduced into the Union, but are not intended to be placed on the market of the Union, from entering into circulation if there are sufficient grounds to suspect that those products are falsified.

2   In order to establish what the necessary measures referred to in paragraph 1 of this Article are, the Commission may adopt, by means of delegated acts in accordance with Article 121a, and subject to the conditions laid down in Articles 121b and 121c, measures supplementing paragraph 1 of this Article as regards the criteria to be considered and the verifications to be made when assessing the potential falsified character of medicinal products introduced into the Union but not intended to be placed on the market.

Article 53

The provisions of this Title shall also apply to homeopathic medicinal products.

4

UK Legislation on the Manufacture, Importation and Distribution of Active Substances

Contents

The Human Medicines Regulations 2012 (SI 2012/1916)

> **Editor's note** These extracts from the Human Medicines Regulations 2012 [SI 2012/1916] as amended by the Human Medicines (Amendment) Regulations 2013 [SI 2013/1855] are presented for the reader's convenience. Reproduction is with the permission of HMSO and the Queen's Printer for Scotland. For any definitive information reference must be made to the original Regulations. The numbering and content within this section corresponds with the regulations set out in the published Statutory Instrument (SI 2012 No. 1916) as amended.

Citation and Commencement

1 (1) These Regulations may be cited as the Human Medicines Regulations 2012.

(2) These Regulations come into force on 14th August 2012.

General Interpretation

8 (1) In these Regulations (unless the context otherwise requires)-

"active substance" means any substance or mixture of substances intended to be used in the manufacture of a medicinal product and that, when used in its production, becomes an active ingredient of that product intended to exert a pharmacological, immunological or metabolic action with a view to restoring, correcting or modifying physiological functions or to make a medical diagnosis;

"assemble", in relation to a medicinal product or an active substance, includes the various processes of dividing up, packaging and presentation of the product or substance, and "assembly" has a corresponding meaning;

"excipient" means any constituent of a medicinal product other than the active substance and the packaging material;

"export" means export, or attempt to export, from the United Kingdom, whether by land, sea or air;

"falsified medicinal product" means any medicinal product with a false representation of:

(a) its identity, including its packaging and labelling, its name or its composition (other than any unintentional quality defect) as regards any of its ingredients including excipients and the strength of those ingredients;

(b) its source, including its manufacturer, its country of manufacturing, its country of origin or its marketing authorisation holder; or

(c) its history, including the records and documents relating to the distribution channels used;

"import" means import, or attempt to import, into the United Kingdom, whether by land, sea or air;

(8) References in these Regulations to:

(a) good manufacturing practice for active substances relate to the principles and guidelines for good manufacturing practice adopted by the European Commission under the third paragraph of Article 47[1] of the 2001 Directive;

(b) good distribution practice for active substances relate to the guidelines on good distribution practices for active substances adopted by the European Commission under the fourth paragraph of Article 47 of the 2001 Directive.

---

[1] Paragraphs 3 and 4 of Article 47 were substituted by Directive 2011/62/EU of the European Parliament and of the Council (OJ No L 174, 1.7.2011, p74).

Chapter 1 Manufacture and Distribution of Medicinal Products and Active Substances

INTERPRETATION

A17. In this Part "manufacture", in relation to an active substance, includes any process carried out in the course of making the substance and the various processes of dividing up, packaging, and presentation of the active substance.

Chapter 4 Importation, Manufacture and Distribution of Active Substances

CRITERIA FOR IMPORTATION, MANUFACTURE OR DISTRIBUTION OF ACTIVE SUBSTANCES

45M. (1) A person may not:
   (a) import;
   (b) manufacture; or
   (c) distribute,
   an active substance unless that person is registered with the licensing authority in accordance with regulation 45N and the requirements in regulation 45O are met.
   (2) Paragraph (1) applies in relation to an active substance which is to be used in an investigational medicinal product only:
   (a) if the product has a marketing authorisation, Article 126a authorisation, certificate of registration or traditional herbal registration; and
   (b) to the extent that the manufacture of the active substance is in accordance with the terms and conditions of that authorisation, certificate or registration.
   (3) Paragraph (1)(a) does not apply to a person who, in connection with the importation of an active substance from a state other than an EEA state:
   (a) provides facilities solely for transporting the active substance; or
   (b) acting as an import agent, imports the active substance solely to the order of another person who holds a certificate of good manufacturing practice issued by the licensing authority.

Registration in Relation to Active Substances

45N. (1) For registration in relation to active substances, the licensing authority must have received a valid registration form from the applicant for import, manufacture or, as the case may be, distribution of the active substance and:

(a) 60 days have elapsed since receipt and the licensing authority have not notified the applicant that an inspection will be carried out; or

(b) the licensing authority:

    (i) notified the applicant within 60 days of receipt of a registration form that an inspection will be carried out; and

    (ii) within 90 days of that inspection the licensing authority have issued that person with a certificate of good manufacturing practice or, as the case may be, of good distribution practice; and

(c) that person has not instructed the licensing authority to end that person's registration.

(2) The person applying for registration under paragraph (1) must notify the licensing authority of any changes which have taken place as regards the information in the registration form:

(a) immediately where such changes may have an impact on quality or safety of the active substances that are manufactured, imported or distributed;

(b) in any other case, on each anniversary of the receipt of the application form by the licensing authority.

(3) For the purpose of paragraph (2), changes which are notified in accordance with that paragraph shall be treated as incorporated in the application form.

(4) Any notification to the licensing authority under paragraph (2) must be accompanied by the appropriate fee in accordance with the Fees Regulations.

(5) A registration form is valid for the purpose of paragraph (1) if:

(a) it is provided to the licensing authority; and

(b) is completed in the way and form specified in Schedule 7A.

(6) Paragraph (1) does not apply until 20th October 2013 in relation to a person who had, before 20th August 2013, commenced the activity for which the person would, apart from this provision, need to send a registration form to the licensing authority.

Requirements for Registration as an Importer, Manufacturer or Distributor of an Active Substance

45O. (1) Where the Commission has adopted principles and guidelines of good manufacturing practice under the third paragraph of Article 47[2] of the 2001 Directive which applies to an active substance manufactured in the UK, the manufacturer must comply with good manufacturing practice in relation to that active substance.

---

[2] Article 47 was amended by Directive 2011/62/EU of the European Parliament and of the Council (OJ No L 174, 1.7.2011, p74).

(2) Where the Commission has adopted principles and guidelines of good distribution practice under the fourth paragraph of Article 47 of the 2001 Directive which applies to an active substance distributed in the United Kingdom, the distributor must comply with good distribution practice in relation to that active substance.

(3) Without prejudice to regulation 37(4) (manufacture and assembly in relation to active substances) and paragraph 9A of Schedule 8 (material to accompany an application for a UK marketing authorisation in relation to an active substance), where the Commission has adopted principles and guidelines of good manufacturing practice under the third paragraph of Article 47 of the 2001 Directive which applies to an active substance imported into the UK and where an active substance is imported from a third country:

(a) the importer must comply with good manufacturing practice and good distribution practice in relation to the active substance;

(b) the active substances must have been manufactured in accordance with standards which are at least equivalent to good manufacturing practice; and

(c) the active substances must be accompanied by a written confirmation from the competent authority of the exporting third country of the following:

(i) the standards of manufacturing practice applicable to the plant manufacturing the exported active substance are at least equivalent to good manufacturing practice,

(ii) the manufacturing plant concerned is subject to regular, strict and transparent controls and to the effective enforcement of standards of manufacturing practice at least equivalent to good manufacturing practice, including repeated and unannounced inspections, so as to ensure a protection of public health at least equivalent to that in the Union, and

(iii) in the event of findings relating to non-compliance, information on such findings is supplied by the exporting third country to the Union without any delay.

(4) Paragraph (3)(c) does not apply:

(a) where the country from where the active substance is exported is included in the list referred to in Article 111b of the 2001 Directive; or

(b) for a period not exceeding the validity of the certificate of good manufacturing practice, where:

(i) in relation to a plant where active substances are manufactured where the competent authority of a member State has found, upon inspection, that a plant complies with the principles and guidelines of good manufacturing practice, and

UK LEGISLATION ON
ACTIVE SUBSTANCES

          (ii) the licensing authority is of the opinion that it is necessary to waive the requirement to ensure availability of the active substance.

(5) The criteria in this regulation apply regardless of whether an active substance is intended for export.

Provision of Information

45P. (1) In this regulation:

"R" means a person who is, or has applied to the licensing authority to become, a registered importer, manufacturer or distributor of active substances;

"reporting year" means a period of twelve months ending on 31st March.

(2) On or before the date specified in paragraph (3), R must submit a report to the licensing authority which:

(a) includes a declaration that R has in place an appropriate system to ensure compliance with regulations 45N, 45O and this regulation; and

(b) details the system which R has in place to ensure such compliance.

(3) The date specified for the purposes of this paragraph is:

(a) in relation to any application made before 31st March 2014, the date of the application; and

(b) in relation to each subsequent reporting year, 30th April following the end of that year.

(4) R must without delay notify the licensing authority of any changes to the matters in respect of which evidence has been supplied in relation to paragraph (2) which might affect compliance with the requirements of this Chapter.

(5) Any report or notification to the licensing authority under paragraph (2) or (4) must be accompanied by the appropriate fee in accordance with the Fees Regulations.

(6) The licensing authority may give a notice to R, requiring R to provide information of a kind specified in the notice within the period specified in the notice.

(7) A notice under paragraph (6) may not be given to R unless it appears to the licensing authority that it is necessary for the licensing authority to consider whether the registration should be varied, suspended or removed from the active substance register.

(8) A notice under paragraph (6) may specify information which the licensing authority thinks necessary for considering whether the registration should be varied, suspended or removed from the active substance register.

Schedule 7A - Information to be Provided for Registration as an Importer, Manufacturer or Distributor of Active Substances

(1) The name and address of the applicant.

(2) The name and address of the person (if any) making the application on the applicant's behalf.

(3) The address of each of the premises where any operations to which the registration relates are to be carried out.

(4) The address of any premises not mentioned by virtue of the above requirement, where:

(a) the applicant proposes to keep any living animals, from which substance(s) used in the production of the active substance(s) to which the application relates are to be derived;

(b) materials of animal origin from which an active substance is to be derived, as mentioned in the above sub-paragraph, are to be kept.

(5) The address of each of the premises where active substances are to be stored, or from which active substances are to be distributed.

(6) The address of each of the premises where any testing associated with the manufacture or assembly of active substances to which the registration relates.

(7) The name, address, qualifications and experience of the person whose duty it will be to supervise any manufacturing operations, and the name and job title of the person to whom they report.

(8) The name, address, qualifications and experience of the person who will have responsibility for the quality control of active substances, and the name and job title of the person to whom they report.

(9) The name, address, qualifications and experience of the person whose duty it will be to supervise any importation, storage or distribution operations, and the name and job title of the person to whom they report.

(10) The name, address and qualifications of the person to be responsible for any animals kept as mentioned in paragraph 4(a).

(11) The name, address and qualifications of the person to be responsible for the culture of any living tissue for use in the manufacture of an active substance.

(12) For each active substance to be manufactured, imported, or distributed:

(a) the CAS registration number[3] assigned to that active substance by the Chemical Abstracts Service, a division of the American Chemical Society;

---

[3] Further information is available from the website of the Chemical Abstracts Service at www.cas.org.

(b) where applicable, the Anatomical Therapeutic Category code[4] assigned to that active substance under the Anatomical Therapeutic Chemical Classification System used for the classification of drugs by the World Health Organisation's Collaborating Centre for Drug Statistics Methodology;

(c) either:

(i) the International Union of Pure and Applied Chemistry nomenclature, or

(ii) the common name; and

(d) the intended quantities of each active substance to be manufactured, imported or distributed.

(13) Details of the operations to which the registration relates, including a statement of whether they include:

(a) the manufacture of active substances;

(b) the importation of active substances from third countries;

(c) the storage of active substances; or

(d) the distribution of active substances.

(14) A statement of the facilities and equipment available at each of the premises where active substances are to be manufactured, stored or distributed.

(15) A statement as to whether the particular active substances are intended for:

(a) use in a medicinal product with an EU marketing authorisation;

(b) use in a special medicinal product; or

(c) export to a third country.

(16) A separate statement in respect of each of the premises mentioned in the application of:

(a) the manufacturing, storage or distribution operations carried out at those sites, and the specific active substances to which those activities relate; and

(b) the equipment available at those premises for carrying out those activities.

(17) A statement of the authority conferred on the person responsible for quality control to reject unsatisfactory active substances.

(18) A description of the arrangements for the identification and storage of materials before and during the manufacture of active substances.

(19) A description of the arrangements for the identification and storage of active substances.

(20) A description of the arrangements at each of the premises where the applicant proposes to store active substances for ensuring, as far as practicable, the turn-over of stocks of active substances.

---

[4] Further information is available from the website of the WHO Collaborating Centre for Drug Statistics Methodology at www.whocc.no.

(21) A description of the arrangements for maintaining:
   (a) production records, including records of manufacture and assembly;
   (b) records of analytical and other tests used in the course of manufacture or assembly for ensuring compliance of materials used in manufacture, or of active substances, with the specification for such materials or active substances;
   (c) records of importation;
   (d) records of storage and distribution.
(22) A description of the arrangements for keeping reference samples of:
   (a) materials used in the manufacture of active substances; and
   (b) active substances.
(23) Where the application relates to active substances intended for use in an advanced therapy medicinal product, an outline of the arrangements for maintaining records to allow traceability containing sufficient detail to enable the linking of an active substance to the advanced therapy medicinal product it was used in the manufacture of and vice versa.
(24) Details of:
   (a) any manufacturing, importation, storage or distribution operations, other than those to which the application for registration relates, carried on by the applicant on or near each of the premises, and
   (b) the substances or articles to which those operations relate.

Guidance on Wholesale Distribution Practice and Brokering Medicines

Guidelines on Good Distribution Practice of Medicinal Products for Human Use (2013/C 68/01)

Contents

Guidelines on Good Distribution Practice of Medicinal Products for Human Use (2013/C 68/01)

These guidelines are based on Article 84 and Article 85(b)(3) of Directive 2001/83/EC of the European Parliament and of the Council of 6 November 2001 on the Community code relating to medicinal products for human use[1] (Directive 2001/83/EC).

The wholesale distribution of medicinal products is an important activity in integrated supply chain management. Today's distribution network for medicinal products is increasingly complex and involves many players. These guidelines lay down appropriate tools to assist wholesale distributors in conducting their activities and to prevent falsified medicines from entering the legal supply chain. Compliance with these guidelines will ensure control of the distribution chain and consequently maintain the quality and the integrity of medicinal products.

According to Article 1(17) of Directive 2001/83/EC, wholesale distribution of medicinal products is all activities consisting of procuring, holding, supplying or exporting medicinal products, apart from supplying medicinal products to the public. Such activities are carried out with manufacturers or their depositories, importers, other wholesale distributors or with pharmacists and persons authorized or entitled to supply medicinal products to the public in the Member State concerned.

Any person acting as a wholesale distributor has to hold a wholesale distribution authorisation. Article 80(g) of Directive 2001/83/EC provides that distributors must comply with the principle of and guidelines for good distribution practice (GDP).

Possession of a manufacturing authorisation includes authorisation to distribute the medicinal products covered by the authorisation. Manufacturers performing any distribution activities with their own products must therefore comply with GDP.

The definition of wholesale distribution does not depend on whether that distributor is established or operating in specific customs areas, such as in free zones or in free warehouses. All obligations related to wholesale distribution activities (such as exporting, holding or supplying) also apply to these distributors. Relevant sections of these guidelines should also be adhered to by other actors involved in the distribution of medicinal products.

Other actors such as brokers may also play a role in the distribution channel for medicinal products. According to Article 85(b), persons brokering medicinal products must be subject to certain provisions

---

[1] OJ L 311, 28.11.2001, p. 67.

applicable to wholesale distributors, as well as specific provisions on brokering.

Chapter 1 – Quality Management

1.1 Principle

Wholesale distributors must maintain a quality system setting out responsibilities, processes and risk management principles in relation to their activities[2]. All distribution activities should be clearly defined and systematically reviewed. All critical steps of distribution processes and significant changes should be justified and where relevant validated. The quality system is the responsibility of the organisation's management and requires their leadership and active participation and should be supported by staff commitment.

1.2 Quality system

The system for managing quality should encompass the organisational structure, procedures, processes and resources, as well as activities necessary to ensure confidence that the product delivered maintains its quality and integrity and remains within the legal supply chain during storage and/or transportation.

The quality system should be fully documented and its effectiveness monitored. All quality system-related activities should be defined and documented. A quality manual or equivalent documentation approach should be established.

A responsible person should be appointed by the management, who should have clearly specified authority and responsibility for ensuring that a quality system is implemented and maintained.

The management of the distributor should ensure that all parts of the quality system are adequately resourced with competent personnel, and suitable and sufficient premises, equipment and facilities.

The size, structure and complexity of distributor's activities should be taken into consideration when developing or modifying the quality system.

A change control system should be in place. This system should incorporate quality risk management principles, and be proportionate and effective.

The quality system should ensure that:

(i)   medicinal products are procured, held, supplied or exported in a way that is compliant with the requirements of GDP;

---

[2] Article 80(h) of Directive 2001/83/EC.

(ii)   management responsibilities are clearly specified;
(iii) products are delivered to the right recipients within a satisfactory time period;
(iv)   records are made contemporaneously;
(v)   deviations from established procedures are documented and investigated;
(vi)   appropriate corrective and preventive actions (commonly known as CAPA) are taken to correct deviations and prevent them in line with the principles of quality risk management.

1.3   Management of outsourced activities

The quality system should extend to the control and review of any outsourced activities related to the procurement, holding, supply or export of medicinal products. These processes should incorporate quality risk management and include:

(i)   assessing the suitability and competence of the Contract Acceptor to carry out the activity and checking authorisation status, if required;
(ii)   defining the responsibilities and communication processes for the quality-related activities of the parties involved;
(iii) monitoring and review of the performance of the Contract Acceptor, and the identification and implementation of any required improvements on a regular basis.

1.4   Management review and monitoring

The management should have a formal process for reviewing the quality system on a periodic basis. The review should include:

(i)   measurement of the achievement of quality system objectives;
(ii)   assessment of performance indicators that can be used to monitor the effectiveness of processes within the quality system, such as complaints, deviations, CAPA, changes to processes; feedback on outsourced activities; self-assessment processes including risk assessments and audits; and external assessments such as inspections, findings and customer audits;
(iii) emerging regulations, guidance and quality issues that can impact the quality management system;
(iv)   innovations that might enhance the quality system;
(v)   changes in business environment and objectives.

The outcome of each management review of the quality system should be documented in a timely manner and effectively communicated internally.

1.5 Quality risk management

Quality risk management is a systematic process for the assessment, control, communication and review of risks to the quality of medicinal products. It can be applied both proactively and retrospectively.

Quality risk management should ensure that the evaluation of the risk to quality is based on scientific knowledge, experience with the process and ultimately links to the protection of the patient. The level of effort, formality and documentation of the process should be commensurate with the level of risk. Examples of the processes and applications of quality risk management can be found in guideline Q9 of the International Conference on Harmonisation (ICH).

Chapter 2 – Personnel

2.1 Principle

The correct distribution of medicinal products relies upon people. For this reason, there must be sufficient competent personnel to carry out all the tasks for which the wholesale distributor is responsible. Individual responsibilities should be clearly understood by the staff and be recorded.

2.2 Responsible person

The wholesale distributor must designate a person as Responsible Person. The Responsible Person should meet the qualifications and all conditions provided for by the legislation of the Member State concerned[1]. A degree in pharmacy is desirable. The Responsible Person should have appropriate competence and experience as well as knowledge of and training in GDP.

The Responsible Person should fulfil their responsibilities personally and should be continuously contactable. The Responsible Person may delegate duties but not responsibilities.

The written job description of the Responsible Person should define their authority to take decisions with regard to their responsibilities. The wholesale distributor should give the Responsible Person the defined authority, resources and responsibility needed to fulfil their duties.

---

[1] Article 79(b) of Directive 2001/83/EC.

The Responsible Person should carry out their duties in such a way as to ensure that the wholesale distributor can demonstrate GDP compliance and that public service obligations are met.

The responsibilities of the Responsible Person include:

(i)   ensuring that a quality management system is implemented and maintained;

(ii)   focusing on the management of authorised activities and the accuracy and quality of records;

(iii) ensuring that initial and continuous training programmes are implemented and maintained;

(iv)   coordinating and promptly performing any recall operations for medicinal products;

(v)   ensuring that relevant customer complaints are dealt with effectively;

(vi)   ensuring that suppliers and customers are approved;

(vii) approving any subcontracted activities which may impact on GDP;

(viii) ensuring that self-inspections are performed at appropriate regular intervals following a prearranged programme and necessary corrective measures are put in place;

(ix)   keeping appropriate records of any delegated duties;

(x)   deciding on the final disposition of returned, rejected, recalled or falsified products;

(xi)   approving any returns to saleable stock;

(xii) ensuring that any additional requirements imposed on certain products by national law are adhered to[2].

2.3 Other personnel

There should be an adequate number of competent personnel involved in all stages of the wholesale distribution activities of medicinal products. The number of personnel required will depend on the volume and scope of activities.

The organisational structure of the wholesale distributor should be set out in an organisation chart. The role, responsibilities, and interrelationships of all personnel should be clearly indicated.

The role and responsibilities of employees working in key positions should be set out in written job descriptions, along with any arrangements for deputising.

---

[2] Article 83 of Directive 2001/83/EC.

2.4 Training

All personnel involved in wholesale distribution activities should be trained on the requirements of GDP. They should have the appropriate competence and experience prior to commencing their tasks.

Personnel should receive initial and continuing training relevant to their role, based on written procedures and in accordance with a written training programme. The Responsible Person should also maintain their competence in GDP through regular training.

In addition, training should include aspects of product identification and avoidance of falsified medicines entering the supply chain.

Personnel dealing with any products which require more stringent handling conditions should receive specific training. Examples of such products include hazardous products, radioactive materials, products presenting special risks of abuse (including narcotic and psychotropic substances), and temperature-sensitive products.

A record of all training should be kept, and the effectiveness of training should be periodically assessed and documented.

2.5 Hygiene

Appropriate procedures relating to personnel hygiene, relevant to the activities being carried out, should be established and observed. Such procedures should cover health, hygiene and clothing.

Chapter 3 – Premises and Equipment

3.1 Principle

Wholesale distributors must have suitable and adequate premises, installations and equipment[1], so as to ensure proper storage and distribution of medicinal products. In particular, the premises should be clean, dry and maintained within acceptable temperature limits.

3.2 Premises

The premises should be designed or adapted to ensure that the required storage conditions are maintained. They should be suitably secure, structurally sound and of sufficient capacity to allow safe storage and handling of the medicinal products. Storage areas should be provided with

EU GDP CHAPTER 3
PREMISES AND
EQUIPMENT

---

[1] Article 79(a) of Directive 2001/83/EC.

adequate lighting to enable all operations to be carried out accurately and safely.

Where premises are not directly operated by the wholesale distributor, a contract should be in place. The contracted premises should be covered by a separate wholesale distribution authorisation.

Medicinal products should be stored in segregated areas which are clearly marked and have access restricted to authorised personnel. Any system replacing physical segregation, such as electronic segregation based on a computerised system, should provide equivalent security and should be validated.

Products pending a decision as to their disposition or products that have been removed from saleable stock should be segregated either physically or through an equivalent electronic system. This includes, for example, any product suspected of falsification and returned products. Medicinal products received from a third country but not intended for the Union market should also be physically segregated. Any falsified medicinal products, expired products, recalled products and rejected products found in the supply chain should be immediately physically segregated and stored in a dedicated area away from all other medicinal products. The appropriate degree of security should be applied in these areas to ensure that such items remain separate from saleable stock. These areas should be clearly identified.

Special attention should be paid to the storage of products with specific handling instructions as specified in national law. Special storage conditions (and special authorisations) may be required for such products (e.g. narcotics and psychotropic substances).

Radioactive materials and other hazardous products, as well as products presenting special safety risks of fire or explosion (e.g. medicinal gases, combustibles, flammable liquids and solids), should be stored in one or more dedicated areas subject to local legislation and appropriate safety and security measures.

Receiving and dispatch bays should protect products from prevailing weather conditions. There should be adequate separation between the receipt and dispatch and storage areas. Procedures should be in place to maintain control of inbound/outbound goods. Reception areas where deliveries are examined following receipt should be designated and suitably equipped.

Unauthorised access to all areas of the authorised premises should be prevented. Prevention measures would usually include a monitored intruder alarm system and appropriate access control. Visitors should be accompanied.

Premises and storage facilities should be clean and free from litter and dust. Cleaning programmes, instructions and records should be in place.

Appropriate cleaning equipment and cleaning agents should be chosen and used so as not to present a source of contamination.

Premises should be designed and equipped so as to afford protection against the entry of insects, rodents or other animals. A preventive pest control programme should be in place.

Rest, wash and refreshment rooms for employees should be adequately separated from the storage areas. The presence of food, drink, smoking material or medicinal products for personal use should be prohibited in the storage areas.

3.2.1. TEMPERATURE AND ENVIRONMENT CONTROL

Suitable equipment and procedures should be in place to check the environment where medicinal products are stored. Environmental factors to be considered include temperature, light, humidity and cleanliness of the premises.

An initial temperature mapping exercise should be carried out on the storage area before use, under representative conditions. Temperature monitoring equipment should be located according to the results of the mapping exercise, ensuring that monitoring devices are positioned in the areas that experience the extremes of fluctuations. The mapping exercise should be repeated according to the results of a risk assessment exercise or whenever significant modifications are made to the facility or the temperature controlling equipment. For small premises of a few square meters which are at room temperature, an assessment of potential risks (e.g. heaters) should be conducted and temperature monitors placed accordingly.

EU GDP CHAPTER 3
PREMISES AND
EQUIPMENT

3.3 Equipment

All equipment impacting on storage and distribution of medicinal products should be designed, located and maintained to a standard which suits its intended purpose. Planned maintenance should be in place for key equipment vital to the functionality of the operation.

Equipment used to control or to monitor the environment where the medicinal products are stored should be calibrated at defined intervals based on a risk and reliability assessment.

Calibration of equipment should be traceable to a national or international measurement standard. Appropriate alarm systems should be in place to provide alerts when there are excursions from predefined storage conditions. Alarm levels should be appropriately set and alarms should be regularly tested to ensure adequate functionality.

Equipment repair, maintenance and calibration operations should be carried out in such a way that the integrity of the medicinal products is not compromised.

Adequate records of repair, maintenance and calibration activities for key equipment should be made and the results should be retained. Key equipment would include for example cold stores, monitored intruder alarm and access control systems, refrigerators, thermo hygrometers, or other temperature and humidity recording devices, air handling units and any equipment used in conjunction with the onward supply chain.

3.3.1. COMPUTERISED SYSTEMS

Before a computerised system is brought into use, it should be demonstrated, through appropriate validation or verification studies, that the system is capable of achieving the desired results accurately, consistently and reproducibly.

A written, detailed description of the system should be available (including diagrams where appropriate). This should be kept up to date. The document should describe principles, objectives, security measures, system scope and main features, how the computerised system is used and the way it interacts with other systems.

Data should only be entered into the computerised system or amended by persons authorised to do so.

Data should be secured by physical or electronic means and protected against accidental or unauthorised modifications. Stored data should be checked periodically for accessibility. Data should be protected by backing up at regular intervals. Backup data should be retained for the period stated in national legislation but at least 5 years at a separate and secure location.

Procedures to be followed if the system fails or breaks down should be defined. This should include systems for the restoration of data.

3.3.2. QUALIFICATION AND VALIDATION

Wholesale distributors should identify what key equipment qualification and/or key process validation is necessary to ensure correct installation and operation. The scope and extent of such qualification and/or validation activities (such as storage, pick and pack processes) should be determined using a documented risk assessment approach.

Equipment and processes should be respectively qualified and/or validated before commencing use and after any significant changes (e.g. repair or maintenance).

Validation and qualification reports should be prepared summarising the results obtained and commenting on any observed deviations. Deviations from established procedures should be documented and further actions decided to correct deviations and avoid their reoccurrence (corrective and preventive actions). The principles of CAPA should be applied where necessary. Evidence of satisfactory validation and acceptance of a process or piece of equipment should be produced and approved by appropriate personnel.

Chapter 4 – Documentation

4.1 Principle

Good documentation constitutes an essential part of the quality system. Written documentation should prevent errors from spoken communication and permits the tracking of relevant operations during the distribution of medicinal products.

4.2 General

Documentation comprises all written procedures, instructions, contracts, records and data, in paper or in electronic form. Documentation should be readily available/retrievable.

With regard to the processing of personal data of employees, complainants or any other natural person, Directive 95/46/EC on the protection of individuals applies to the processing of personal data and to the free movement of such data.

Documentation should be sufficiently comprehensive with respect to the scope of the wholesale distributor's activities and in a language understood by personnel. It should be written in clear, unambiguous language and be free from errors.

Procedures should be approved signed and dated by the responsible person. Documentation should be approved, signed and dated by appropriate authorised persons, as required. It should not be handwritten; although, where it is necessary, sufficient space should be provided for such entries.

Any alteration made in the documentation should be signed and dated; the alteration should permit the reading of the original information. Where appropriate, the reason for the alteration should be recorded.

Documents should be retained for the period stated in national legislation but at least 5 years. Personal data should be deleted or anonymised as soon as their storage is no longer than necessary for the purpose of distribution activities.

Each employee should have ready access to all necessary documentation for the tasks executed.

Attention should be paid to using valid and approved procedures. Documents should have unambiguous content; title, nature and purpose should be clearly stated. Documents should be reviewed regularly and kept up to date. Version control should be applied to procedures. After revision of a document a system should exist to prevent inadvertent use of the superseded version. Superseded or obsolete procedures should be removed from workstations and archived.

Records must be kept either in the form of purchase/sales invoices, delivery slips, or on computer or any other form, for any transaction in medicinal products received, supplied or brokered.

Records must include at least the following information: date; name of the medicinal product; quantity received, supplied or brokered; name and address of the supplier, customer, broker or consignee, as appropriate; and batch number at least for medicinal product bearing the safety features[1].

Records should be made at the time each operation is undertaken.

Chapter 5 — Operations

5.1 Principle

All actions taken by wholesale distributors should ensure that the identity of the medicinal product is not lost and that the wholesale distribution of medicinal products is performed according to the information on the outer packaging. The wholesale distributor should use all means available to minimise the risk of falsified medicinal products entering the legal supply chain.

All medicinal products distributed in the EU by a wholesale distributor must be covered by a marketing authorisation granted by the EU or by a Member State[2].

Any distributor, other than the marketing authorisation holder, who imports a medicinal product from another Member State must notify the marketing authorisation holder and the competent authority in the Member State to which the medicinal product will be imported of their intention to import that product[3]. All key operations described below should be fully described in the quality system in appropriate documentation.

5.2 Qualification of suppliers

Wholesale distributors must obtain their supplies of medicinal products only from persons who are themselves in possession of a wholesale

---

[1] Articles 80(e) and 82 of Directive 2001/83/EC.
[2] Articles 76(1) and (2) of Directive 2001/83/EC.
[3] Article 76(3) of Directive 2001/83/EC.

distribution authorisation, or who are in possession of a manufacturing authorisation which covers the product in question[4].

Wholesale distributors receiving medicinal products from third countries for the purpose of importation, i.e. for the purpose of placing these products on the EU market, must hold a manufacturing authorisation[5].

Where medicinal products are obtained from another wholesale distributor the receiving wholesale distributor must verify that the supplier complies with the principles and guidelines of good distribution practices and that they hold an authorisation for example by using the Union database. If the medicinal product is obtained through brokering, the wholesale distributor must verify that the broker is registered and complies with the requirements in Chapter 10[1].

Appropriate qualification and approval of suppliers should be performed prior to any procurement of medicinal products. This should be controlled by a procedure and the results documented and periodically rechecked.

When entering into a new contract with new suppliers the wholesale distributor should carry out 'due diligence' checks in order to assess the suitability, competence and reliability of the other party. Attention should be paid to:

(i)   the reputation or reliability of the supplier;
(ii)   offers of medicinal products more likely to be falsified;
(iii) large offers of medicinal products which are generally only available in limited quantities; and
(iv)   out-of-range prices.

5.3 Qualification of customers

Wholesale distributors must ensure they supply medicinal products only to persons who are themselves in possession of a wholesale distribution authorisation or who are authorised or entitled to supply medicinal products to the public.

Checks and periodic rechecks may include: requesting copies of customer's authorisations according to national law, verifying status on an authority website, requesting evidence of qualifications or entitlement according to national legislation.

---

[4] Article 80(b) of Directive 2001/83/EC.
[5] Article 40, third paragraph of Directive 2001/83/EC.
[1] Article 80, fourth paragraph of Directive 2001/83/EC.

EU GDP CHAPTER 5 OPERATIONS

Wholesale distributors should monitor their transactions and investigate any irregularity in the sales patterns of narcotics, psychotropic substances or other dangerous substances. Unusual sales patterns that may constitute diversion or misuse of medicinal product should be investigated and reported to competent authorities where necessary. Steps should be taken to ensure fulfilment of any public service obligation imposed upon them.

5.4   Receipt of medicinal products

The purpose of the receiving function is to ensure that the arriving consignment is correct, that the medicinal products originate from approved suppliers and that they have not been visibly damaged during transport.

Medicinal products requiring special storage or security measures should be prioritised and once appropriate checks have been conducted they should be immediately transferred to appropriate storage facilities.

Batches of medicinal products intended for the EU and EEA countries should not be transferred to saleable stock before assurance has been obtained in accordance with written procedures, that they are authorised for sale. For batches coming from another Member State, prior to their transfer to saleable stock, the control report referred to in Article 51(1) of Directive 2001/83/EC or another proof of release to the market in question based on an equivalent system should be carefully checked by appropriately trained personnel.

5.5   Storage

Medicinal products and, if necessary, healthcare products should be stored separately from other products likely to alter them and should be protected from the harmful effects of light, temperature, moisture and other external factors. Particular attention should be paid to products requiring specific storage conditions.

Incoming containers of medicinal products should be cleaned, if necessary, before storage.

Warehousing operations must ensure appropriate storage conditions are maintained and allow for appropriate security of stocks.

Stock should be rotated according to the first expiry, first out (FEFO) principle. Exceptions should be documented.

Medicinal products should be handled and stored in such a manner as to prevent spillage, breakage, contamination and mix-ups. Medicinal products should not be stored directly on the floor unless the package is designed to allow such storage (such as for some medicinal gas cylinders).

Medicinal products that are nearing or are beyond their expiry date/shelf life should be withdrawn immediately from saleable stock either physically or through other equivalent electronic segregation.

Stock inventories should be performed regularly taking into account national legislation requirements. Stock irregularities should be investigated and documented.

5.6   Destruction of obsolete goods

Medicinal products intended for destruction should be appropriately identified, held separately and handled in accordance with a written procedure.

Destruction of medicinal products should be in accordance with national or international requirements for handling, transport and disposal of such products.

Records of all destroyed medicinal products should be retained for a defined period.

5.7   Picking

Controls should be in place to ensure the correct product is picked. The product should have an appropriate remaining shelf life when it is picked.

5.8   Supply

For all supplies, a document (e.g. delivery note) must be enclosed stating the date; name and pharmaceutical form of the medicinal product, batch number at least for products bearing the safety features; quantity supplied; name and address of the supplier, name and delivery address of the consignee[1] (actual physical storage premises, if different) and applicable transport and storage conditions. Records should be kept so that the actual location of the product can be known.

5.9   Export to third countries

The export of medicinal products falls within the definition of 'wholesale distribution'[2]. A person exporting medicinal products must hold a wholesale distribution authorisation or a manufacturing authorisation.

---

[1] Article 82 of Directive 2001/83/EC.
[2] Article 1(17) of Directive 2001/83/EC.

EU GDP CHAPTER 5
OPERATIONS

This is also the case if the exporting wholesale distributor is operating from a free zone.

The rules for wholesale distribution apply in their entirety in the case of export of medicinal products. However, where medicinal products are exported, they do not need to be covered by a marketing authorisation of the Union or a Member State[3]. Wholesalers should take the appropriate measures in order to prevent these medicinal products reaching the Union market. Where wholesale distributors supply medicinal products to persons in third countries, they shall ensure that such supplies are only made to persons who are authorised or entitled to receive medicinal products for wholesale distribution or supply to the public in accordance with the applicable legal and administrative provisions of the country concerned.

Chapter 6 – Complaints, Returns, Suspected Falsified Medicinal Products and Medicinal Product Recalls

6.1 Principle

All complaints, returns, suspected falsified medicinal products and recalls must be recorded and handled carefully according to written procedures. Records should be made available to the competent authorities. An assessment of returned medicinal products should be performed before any approval for resale. A consistent approach by all partners in the supply chain is required in order to be successful in the fight against falsified medicinal products.

6.2 Complaints

Complaints should be recorded with all the original details. A distinction should be made between complaints related to the quality of a medicinal product and those related to distribution. In the event of a complaint about the quality of a medicinal product and a potential product defect, the manufacturer and/or marketing authorisation holder should be informed without delay. Any product distribution complaint should be thoroughly investigated to identify the origin of or reason for the complaint.

A person should be appointed to handle complaints and allocated sufficient support personnel.

If necessary, appropriate follow-up actions (including CAPA) should be taken after investigation and evaluation of the complaint, including where required notification to the national competent authorities.

---

[3] Article 85(a) of Directive 2001/83/EC.

6.3 Returned medicinal products

Returned products must be handled according to a written, risk-based process taking into account the product concerned, any specific storage requirements and the time elapsed since the medicinal product was originally dispatched. Returns should be conducted in accordance with national law and contractual arrangements between the parties.

Medicinal products which have left the premises of the distributor should only be returned to saleable stock if all of the following are confirmed:

(i)   the medicinal products are in their unopened and undamaged secondary packaging and are in good condition; have not expired and have not been recalled;

(ii) medicinal products returned from a customer not holding a wholesale distribution authorisation or from pharmacies authorised to supply medicinal products to the public should always be returned to saleable stock if they are returned within an acceptable time limit, for example 10 days.

(iii) it has been demonstrated by the customer that the medicinal products have been transported, stored and handled in compliance with their specific storage requirements;

(iv) they have been examined and assessed by a sufficiently trained and competent person authorised to do so;

(v)   the distributor has reasonable evidence that the product was supplied to that customer (via copies of the original delivery note or by referencing invoice numbers, etc.) and the batch number for products bearing the safety features is known, and that there is no reason to believe that the product has been falsified.

Moreover, for medicinal products requiring specific temperature storage conditions such as low temperature, returns to saleable stock can only be made if there is documented evidence that the product has been stored under the authorised storage conditions throughout the entire time. If any deviation has occurred a risk assessment has to be performed, on which basis the integrity of the product can be demonstrated. The evidence should cover:

(i)   delivery to customer;
(ii) examination of the product;
(iii) opening of the transport packaging;
(iv) return of the product to the packaging;
(v)   collection and return to the distributor;
(vi) return to the distribution site refrigerator.

EU GDP CHAPTER 6
COMPLAINTS, RETURNS,
SUSPECTED FALSIFIED
MEDICINAL PRODUCTS

Products returned to saleable stock should be placed such that the 'first expired first out' (FEFO) system operates effectively.

Stolen products that have been recovered cannot be returned to saleable stock and sold to customers.

6.4 Falsified medicinal products

Wholesale distributors must immediately inform the competent authority and the marketing authorisation holder of any medicinal products they identify as falsified or suspect to be falsified[1]. A procedure should be in place to this effect. It should be recorded with all the original details and investigated.

Any falsified medicinal products found in the supply chain should immediately be physically segregated and stored in a dedicated area away from all other medicinal products. All relevant activities in relation to such products should be documented and records retained.

6.5 Medicinal product recalls

The effectiveness of the arrangements for product recall should be evaluated regularly (at least annually).

Recall operations should be capable of being initiated promptly and at any time.

The distributor must follow the instructions of a recall message, which should be approved, if required, by the competent authorities.

Any recall operation should be recorded at the time it is carried out. Records should be made readily available to the competent authorities.

The distribution records should be readily accessible to the person(s) responsible for the recall, and should contain sufficient information on distributors and directly supplied customers (with addresses, phone and/or fax numbers inside and outside working hours, batch numbers at least for medicinal products bearing safety features as required by legislation and quantities delivered), including those for exported products and medicinal product samples.

The progress of the recall process should be recorded for a final report.

---

[1] Article 80(i) of Directive 2001/83/EC.

Chapter 7 — Outsourced Activities

7.1   Principle

Any activity covered by the GDP Guide that is outsourced should be correctly defined, agreed and controlled in order to avoid misunderstandings which could affect the integrity of the product. There must be a written Contract between the Contract Giver and the Contract Acceptor which clearly establishes the duties of each party.

7.2   Contract giver

The Contract Giver is responsible for the activities contracted out.

The Contract Giver is responsible for assessing the competence of the Contract Acceptor to successfully carry out the work required and for ensuring by means of the contract and through audits that the principles and guidelines of GDP are followed. An audit of the Contract Acceptor should be performed before commencement of, and whenever there has been a change to, the outsourced activities. The frequency of audit should be defined based on risk depending on the nature of the outsourced activities. Audits should be permitted at any time.

The Contract Giver should provide the Contract Acceptor with all the information necessary to carry out the contracted operations in accordance with the specific product requirements and any other relevant requirements.

7.3   Contract acceptor

The Contract Acceptor should have adequate premises and equipment, procedures, knowledge and experience, and competent personnel to carry out the work ordered by the Contract Giver.

The Contract Acceptor should not pass to a third party any of the work entrusted to him under the contract without the Contract Giver's prior evaluation and approval of the arrangements and an audit of the third party by the Contract Giver or the Contract Acceptor. Arrangements made between the Contract Acceptor and any third party should ensure that the wholesale distribution information is made available in the same way as between the original Contract Giver and Contract Acceptor.

The Contract Acceptor should refrain from any activity which may adversely affect the quality of the product(s) handled for the Contract Giver.

The Contract Acceptor must forward any information that can influence the quality of the product(s) to the Contract Giver in accordance with the requirement of the contract.

Chapter 8 – Self-inspections

8.1 Principle

Self-inspections should be conducted in order to monitor implementation and compliance with GDP principles and to propose necessary corrective measures.

8.2 Self-inspections

A self-inspection programme should be implemented covering all aspects of GDP and compliance with the regulations, guidelines and procedures within a defined time frame. Self-inspections may be divided into several individual self-inspections of limited scope.

Self-inspections should be conducted in an impartial and detailed way by designated competent company personnel. Audits by independent external experts may also be useful but may not be used as a substitute for self-inspection.

All self-inspections should be recorded. Reports should contain all the observations made during the inspection. A copy of the report should be provided to the management and other relevant persons. In the event that irregularities and/or deficiencies are observed, their cause should be determined and the corrective and preventive actions (CAPA) should be documented and followed up.

Chapter 9 – Transportation

9.1 Principle

It is the responsibility of the supplying wholesale distributor to protect medicinal products against breakage, adulteration and theft, and to ensure that temperature conditions are maintained within acceptable limits during transport.

Regardless of the mode of transport, it should be possible to demonstrate that the medicines have not been exposed to conditions that may compromise their quality and integrity. A risk-based approach should be utilised when planning transportation.

9.2 Transportation

The required storage conditions for medicinal products should be maintained during transportation within the defined limits as described by the manufacturers or on the outer packaging.

If a deviation such as temperature excursion or product damage has occurred during transportation, this should be reported to the distributor and recipient of the affected medicinal products. A procedure should also be in place for investigating and handling temperature excursions.

It is the responsibility of the wholesale distributor to ensure that vehicles and equipment used to distribute, store or handle medicinal products are suitable for their use and appropriately equipped to prevent exposure of the products to conditions that could affect their quality and packaging integrity.

There should be written procedures in place for the operation and maintenance of all vehicles and equipment involved in the distribution process, including cleaning and safety precautions.

Risk assessment of delivery routes should be used to determine where temperature controls are required. Equipment used for temperature monitoring during transport within vehicles and/or containers, should be maintained and calibrated at regular intervals at least once a year.

Dedicated vehicles and equipment should be used, where possible, when handling medicinal products. Where non-dedicated vehicles and equipment are used procedures should be in place to ensure that the quality of the medicinal product will not be compromised.

Deliveries should be made to the address stated on the delivery note and into the care or the premises of the consignee. Medicinal products should not be left on alternative premises.

For emergency deliveries outside normal business hours, persons should be designated and written procedures should be available.

Where transportation is performed by a third party, the contract in place should encompass the requirements of Chapter 7. Transportation providers should be made aware by the wholesale distributor of the relevant transport conditions applicable to the consignment. Where the transportation route includes unloading and reloading or transit storage at a transportation hub, particular attention should be paid to temperature monitoring, cleanliness and the security of any intermediate storage facilities.

Provision should be made to minimise the duration of temporary storage while awaiting the next stage of the transportation route.

EU GDP CHAPTER 9
TRANSPORTATION

9.3 Containers, packaging and labelling

Medicinal products should be transported in containers that have no adverse effect on the quality of the products, and that offer adequate protection from external influences, including contamination.

Selection of a container and packaging should be based on the storage and transportation requirements of the medicinal products; the space required for the amount of medicines; the anticipated external temperature extremes; the estimated maximum time for transportation including transit storage at customs; the qualification status of the packaging and the validation status of the shipping containers.

Containers should bear labels providing sufficient information on handling and storage requirements and precautions to ensure that the products are properly handled and secured at all times. The containers should enable identification of the contents of the containers and the source.

9.4 Products requiring special conditions

In relation to deliveries containing medicinal products requiring special conditions such as narcotics or psychotropic substances, the wholesale distributor should maintain a safe and secure supply chain for these products in accordance with requirements laid down by the Member States concerned. There should be additional control systems in place for delivery of these products. There should be a protocol to address the occurrence of any theft.

Medicinal products comprising highly active and radioactive materials should be transported in safe, dedicated and secure containers and vehicles. The relevant safety measures should be in accordance with international agreements and national legislation.

For temperature-sensitive products, qualified equipment (e.g. thermal packaging, temperature-controlled containers or temperature controlled vehicles) should be used to ensure correct transport conditions are maintained between the manufacturer, wholesale distributor and customer.

If temperature-controlled vehicles are used, the temperature monitoring equipment used during transport should be maintained and calibrated at regular intervals. Temperature mapping under representative conditions should be carried out and should take into account seasonal variations.

If requested, customers should be provided with information to demonstrate that products have complied with the temperature storage conditions.

If cool packs are used in insulated boxes, they need to be located such that the product does not come in direct contact with the cool pack. Staff must be trained on the procedures for assembly of the insulated boxes (seasonal configurations) and on the reuse of cool packs.

There should be a system in place to control the reuse of cool packs to ensure that incompletely cooled packs are not used in error. There should be adequate physical segregation between frozen and chilled ice packs.

The process for delivery of sensitive products and control of seasonal temperature variations should be described in a written procedure.

Chapter 10 – Specific Provisions for Brokers[1]

10.1 Principle

A 'broker' is a person involved in activities in relation to the sale or purchase of medicinal products, except for wholesale distribution, that do not include physical handling and that consist of negotiating independently and on behalf of another legal or natural person[2].

Brokers are subject to a registration requirement. They must have a permanent address and contact details in the Member State where they are registered[3]. They must notify the competent authority of any changes to those details without unnecessary delay.

By definition, brokers do not procure, supply or hold medicines. Therefore, requirements for premises, installations and equipment as set out in Directive 2001/83/EC do not apply. However, all other rules in Directive 2001/83/EC that apply to wholesale distributors also apply to brokers.

10.2 Quality system

The quality system of a broker should be defined in writing, approved and kept up to date. It should set out responsibilities, processes and risk management in relation to their activities.

The quality system should include an emergency plan which ensures effective recall of medicinal products from the market ordered by the manufacturer or the competent authorities or carried out in cooperation with the manufacturer or marketing authorisation holder for the medicinal

---

[1] Article 85(b)(3) of Directive 2001/83/EC.
[2] Article 1(17a) of Directive 2001/83/EC.
[3] Article 85(b) of Directive 2001/83/EC.

product concerned[4]. The competent authorities must be immediately informed of any suspected falsified medicines offered in the supply chain[5].

10.3 Personnel

Any member of personnel involved in the brokering activities should be trained in the applicable EU and national legislation and in the issues concerning falsified medicinal products.

10.4 Documentation

The general provisions on documentation in Chapter 4 apply.

In addition, at least the following procedures and instructions, along with the corresponding records of execution, should be in place:

(i)   procedure for complaints handling;

(ii)   procedure for informing competent authorities and marketing authorisation holders of suspected falsified medicinal products;

(iii)   procedure for supporting recalls;

(iv)   procedure for ensuring that medicinal products brokered have a marketing authorisation;

(v)   procedure for verifying that their supplying wholesale distributors hold a distribution authorisation, their supplying manufacturers or importers hold a manufacturing authorisation and their customers are authorised to supply medicinal products in the Member State concerned;

(vi)   records should be kept either in the form of purchase/sales invoices or on computer, or in any other form for any transaction in medicinal products brokered and should contain at least the following information: date; name of the medicinal product; quantity brokered; name and address of the supplier and the customer; and batch number at least for products bearing the safety features.

Records should be made available to the competent authorities, for inspection purposes, for the period stated in national legislation but at least 5 years.

---

[4]   Article 80(d) of Directive 2001/83/EC.
[5]   Article 85(b)(1), third paragraph of Directive 2001/83/EC.

ANNEX

Glossary of terms

Term	Definition
Good Distribution Practice (GDP)	GDP is that part of quality assurance which ensures that the quality of medicinal products is maintained throughout all stages of the supply chain from the site of manufacturer to the pharmacy or person authorised or entitled to supply medicinal products to the public.
Export procedure	Export procedure: Allow Community goods to leave the customs territory of the Union. For the purpose of these guidelines, the supply of medicines from EU Member State to a contracting State of the European Economic Area is not considered as export.
Falsified medicinal product[1]	Any medicinal product with a false representation of: (a) its identity, including its packaging and labelling, its name or its composition as regards any of the ingredients including excipients and the strength of those ingredients; (b) its source, including its manufacturer, its country of manufacturing, its country of origin or its marketing authorisation holder; or (c) its history, including the records and documents relating to the distribution channels used.
Free zones and free warehouses[2]	Free zones and free warehouses are parts of the customs territory of the Community or premises situated in that territory and separated from the rest of it in which: (a) Community goods are considered, for the purpose of import duties and commercial policy import measures, as not being on Community customs territory, provided they are not released for free circulation or placed under another customs procedure or used or consumed under conditions other than those provided for in customs regulations; (b) Community goods for which such provision is made under Community legislation governing specific fields qualify, by virtue of being placed in a free zone or free warehouse, for measures normally attaching to the export of goods.

EU GDP ANNEX

(Continued)

Glossary of terms (*Continued*)

Term	Definition
Holding	Storing medicinal products.
Transport	Moving medicinal products between two locations without storing them for unjustified periods of time.
Procuring	Obtaining, acquiring, purchasing or buying medicinal products from manufacturers, importers or other wholesale distributors.
Qualification	Action of proving that any equipment works correctly and actually leads to the expected results. The word validation is sometimes widened to incorporate the concept of qualification. (Defined in EudraLex Volume 4 Glossary to the GMP Guidelines).
Supplying	All activities of providing, selling, donating medicinal products to wholesalers, pharmacists, or persons authorised or entitled to supply medicinal products to the public.
Quality Risk Management	A systematic process for the assessment, control, communication and review of risks to the quality of the drug (medicinal) product across the product life cycle.
Quality System	The sum of all aspects of a system that implements quality policy and ensures that quality objectives are met. (International Conference on Harmonisation of Technical Requirements for Registration of Pharmaceuticals for Human Use, Q9).
Validation	Action of proving that any procedure, process, equipment, material, activity or system actually leads to the expected results (see also Qualification). (Defined in EudraLex Volume 4 Glossary to the GMP Guidelines)

[1] Article 1(33) of Directive 2001/83/EC.
[2] Articles 166 to Article 181 of Council Regulation (EEC) No 2913/92 of 12 October 1992 establishing the Community Customs Code, (OJ L 302, 19.10.1992, p. 1).

UK Guidance on Wholesale Distribution Practice

Contents

Conditions of Holding a Wholesale Dealer's Licence

The holder of a wholesale dealer's licence must comply with certain conditions in relation to the wholesale distribution of relevant medicinal products. These conditions are set out in Regulations 43 – 45 of the Human Medicines Regulations 2012 [SI 2012/1916] ("the Regulations"). They require that the licence holder shall:

(a) comply with the guidelines on Good Distribution Practice (GDP);[1]

---

[1] Guidelines on Good Distribution Practice of Medicinal Products for Human Use (2013/C 68/01).

(b) ensure, within the limits of his responsibility as a distributor of relevant medicinal products, the appropriate and continued supply of such relevant medicinal products to pharmacies and persons who may lawfully sell such products by retail or who may lawfully supply them in circumstances corresponding to retail sale;

(c) provide and maintain such staff, premises, equipment and facilities for the handling, storage and distribution of the relevant medicinal products which he handles, in accordance with his licence as are necessary to maintain the quality of, and ensure proper distribution of the medicinal products (see Control and Monitoring of Storage and Transportation Temperatures);

(d) inform the licensing authority of any proposed structural alteration to, or discontinued use of, premises to which the licence relates or premises which have been approved by the licensing authority;

(e) inform the licensing authority of any change to the responsible person.

The holder of a wholesale dealer's licence shall not sell or offer for sale or supply any relevant medicinal product unless there is a marketing authorisation, Article 126a authorisation, certificate of registration or traditional herbal registration ("an authorisation") for the time being in force in respect of that product; and the sale or offer for sale is in accordance with the provisions of that authorisation.

The restrictions on the holder of a wholesale dealer's licence shall not apply to:

(a) the sale or offer for sale of a special medicinal product; and

(b) the export to an EEA State, or supply for the purposes of such export, of a medicinal product which may be placed on the market in that State without a marketing authorisation, Article 126a authorisation, certificate of registration or traditional herbal registration by virtue of legislation adopted by that State under Article 5(1) of the 2001 Directive; or

(c) the sale or supply, or offer for sale or supply, of an unauthorised medicinal product where the Secretary of State has temporarily authorised the distribution of the product under regulation 174 of the Regulations.

The holder of a wholesale dealer's licence shall:

(a) keep such documents relating to the sale of medicinal products to which his licence relates as will facilitate the withdrawal or recall from sale of relevant medicinal products in accordance with paragraph (b);

(b) have in place an emergency plan which will ensure effective implementation of the recall from the market of any relevant medicinal products where such recall is:

   (i) ordered by the licensing authority or by the competent authority of
       any other EEA State, or

   (ii) carried out in co-operation with the manufacturer of, or the holder
        of the marketing authorisation for, the product in question;

(c) keep records in relation to the receipt, dispatch or brokering of
    medicinal products, of the date of receipt, the date of despatch, the date
    of brokering, the name of the medicinal product, the quantity of the
    product received, dispatched or brokered, the name and address of the
    person from whom the products were received or to whom they are
    dispatched, and the batch number of medicinal products bearing safety
    features referred to in point (o) of Article 54[2] of the 2001 Directive.

Where the holder of a wholesale dealer's licence imports from another EEA
State for which they are not the holder of the marketing authorisation,
Article 126a authorisation, certificate of registration or a traditional herbal
registration of the product, then they shall notify the holder of that
authorisation of their intention to import that product. In the case where
the product is the subject of a marketing authorisation granted under
Regulation (EC) No 726/2004, the holder of the wholesale dealer's licence
shall notify the EMA or for any other authorisation they the shall notify the
licensing authority. In both cases they will be required to pay a fee to the
EMA in accordance with Article 76(4)[3] of the 2001 Directive or the
licensing authority as the case may be, in accordance with the Fees
Regulations. These requirements will not apply in relation to the wholesale
distribution of medicinal products to a person in a non-EEA country.

   The licence holder, for the purposes of enabling the licensing authority to
determine whether there are grounds for suspending, revoking or varying
the licence, must permit a person authorised in writing by the licensing
authority, on production of identification, to carry out any inspection, or to
take any samples or copies, which an inspector could carry out or take
under Part 16 (enforcement) of the Human Medicines Regulations 2012 [SI
2012/1916].

   The holder of a wholesale dealer's licence must verify that any medicinal
products they receive which are required by Article 54a[4] of the Directive to
bear safety features are not falsified. This does not apply in relation to the
distribution of medicinal products received from a third country by a

UK GUIDANCE ON WHOLESALE DISTRIBUTION PRACTICE

---

[2] Point (o) of Article 54a was inserted by Directive 2011/62/EU of the European
  Parliament and of the Council (OJ No L 174, 1.7.2011, p74).

[3] Article 76(4) was inserted by Directive 2011/62/EU of the European Parliament
  and of the Council (OJ No L 174, 1.7.2011, p74).

[4] Article 54a was inserted by Directive 2011/62/EU of the European Parliament
  and of the Council (OJ No L 174, 1.7.2011, p74).

person for supply to a person in a third country. Any verification is carried out by checking the safety features on the outer packaging, in accordance with the requirements laid down in the delegated acts adopted under Article 54a(2) of the 2001 Directive.

The licence holder must maintain a quality system setting out responsibilities, processes and risk management measures in relation to their activities.

The licence holder must also immediately inform the licensing authority and, where applicable, the marketing authorisation holder, of medicinal products which the licence holder receives or is offered which the licence holder knows or suspects, or has reasonable grounds for knowing or suspecting, to be falsified.

Where the medicinal product is obtained through brokering, the licence holder must verify that the broker involved fulfils the requirements set out in the Human Medicines Regulations 2012 [SI 2012/1916]. (See chapters 8, 10 and 13 of this guide.)

The licence holder must not obtain supplies of medicinal products from anyone except the holder of a manufacturer's licence or wholesale dealer's licence in relation to products of that description or the person who holds an authorisation granted by another EEA State authorising the manufacture of products of the description or their distribution by way of wholesale dealing. The supply must be in accordance with the principles and guidelines of good distribution practice. This does not apply in relation to the distribution of medicinal products directly received from a non-EEA country but not imported into the EU.

From 28th October 2013 where the medicinal product is directly received from a non-EEA country for export to a non-EEA country, the licenced wholesale dealer must check that the supplier of the medicinal product in the exporting non-EEA country is authorised or entitled to supply such medicinal products in accordance with the legal and administrative provisions in that country.

The holder of a wholesale dealer's licence must verify that the wholesale dealer who supplies the product complies with the principles and guidelines of good distribution practices; or the manufacturer or importer who supplies the product holds a manufacturing authorisation.

The holder of a wholesale dealer's licence may distribute medicinal products by way of wholesale dealing only to the holder of a wholesale dealer's licence relating to those products, the holder of an authorisation granted by the competent authority of another EEA State authorising the supply of those products by way of wholesale dealing, a person who may lawfully sell those products by retail or may lawfully supply them in circumstances corresponding to retail sale; or a person who may lawfully administer those products. This does not apply in relation to medicinal products which are distributed by way of wholesale dealing to a person in a non-EEA country.

From 28th October 2013, where the medicinal product is supplied directly to persons in a non-EEA country the licensed wholesale dealer must check that the person that receives it is authorised or entitled to receive medicinal products for wholesale distribution or supply to the public in accordance with the applicable legal and administrative provisions of the non-EEA country concerned.

Where any medicinal product is supplied to any person who may lawfully sell those products by retail or who may lawfully supply them in circumstances corresponding to retail sale, the licence holder shall enclose with the product a document which makes it possible to ascertain:

(a) the date on which the supply took place;
(b) the name and pharmaceutical form of the product supplied;
(c) the quantity of product supplied;
(d) the names and addresses of the person or persons from whom the products were supplied to the licence holder; and
(e) the batch number of the medicinal products bearing the safety features referred to in point (o) of Article 54 of the 2001 Directive.

The holder of a wholesale dealer's licence shall keep a record of the information supplied where any medicinal product is supplied to any person who may lawfully sell those products by retail or who may lawfully supply them in circumstances corresponding to retail sale for a minimum period of five years after the date on which it is supplied and ensure, during that period, that that record is available to the licensing authority for inspection.

The wholesale dealer's licence holder shall at all times have at his disposal the services of a responsible person who, in the opinion of the licensing authority has knowledge of the activities to be carried out and of the procedures to be performed under the licence which is adequate for performing the functions of responsible person; and has experience in those procedures and activities which is adequate for those purposes.

The functions of the responsible person shall be to ensure, in relation to medicinal products, that the conditions under which the licence has been granted have been, and are being, complied with and the quality of medicinal products which are being handled by the wholesale dealer's licence holder are being maintained in accordance with the requirements of the marketing authorisations, Article 126a authorisations, certificates of registration or traditional herbal registrations applicable to those products.

The standard provisions for wholesale dealer's licences, that is, those provisions which may be included in all licences unless the licence specifically provides otherwise, insofar as those licences relate to relevant medicinal products, shall be those provisions set out in Part 4 of Schedule 4 of the Human Medicines Regulations 2012 [SI 2012/1916].

The licence holder shall not use any premises for the purpose of the handling, storage or distribution of relevant medicinal products other than those specified in his licence or notified to the licensing authority by him and approved by the licensing authority.

The licence holder shall provide such information as may be requested by the licensing authority concerning the type and quantity of any relevant medicinal products which he handles, stores or distributes.

Where and insofar as the licence relates to special medicinal products to which regulation 167 of the Human Medicines Regulations 2012 apply which do not have a UK or EMA authorisation and are commonly known as "specials" (refer to Guidance Note 14), the licence holder shall only import such products from another EEA State:

(i) in response to an order which satisfies the requirements of regulation 167 of the Regulations; and

(ii) where the following conditions are complied with:

    (1) No later than 28 days prior to each importation of a special medicinal product, the licence holder shall give written notice to the licensing authority stating his intention to import that special medicinal product and stating the following particulars:

        (a) the name of the medicinal product, being the brand name or the common name, or the scientific name, and any name, if different, under which the medicinal product is to be sold or supplied in the United Kingdom,

        (b) any trademark or name of the manufacturer of the medicinal product;

        (c) in respect of each active constituent of the medicinal product, any international non-proprietary name or the British approved name or the monograph name or, where that constituent does not have an international non-proprietary name, a British approved name or a monograph name, the accepted scientific name or any other name descriptive of the true nature of that constituent;

        (d) the quantity of medicinal product which is to be imported which shall not exceed the quantity specified in subparagraph (5); and

        (f) the name and address of the manufacturer or assembler of that medicinal product in the form in which it is to be imported and, if the person who will supply that medicinal product for importation is not the manufacturer or assembler, the name and address of such supplier.

    (2) Subject to subparagraph (3), the licence holder shall not import the special medicinal product if, before the end of 28 days from the date on which the licensing authority sends or gives the licence

holder an acknowledgement in writing by the licensing authority that they have received the notice referred to in subparagraph (1) above, the licensing authority have notified him in writing that the product should not be imported.

(3) The licence holder may import the special medicinal product referred to in the notice where he has been notified in writing by the licensing authority, before the end of the 28 day period referred to in subparagraph (2), that the special medicinal product may be imported.

(4) Where the licence holder sells or supplies special medicinal products, he shall, in addition to any other records which he is required by the provisions of his licence to make, make and maintain written records relating to:

(i) the batch number of the batch of the product from which the sale or supply was made; and

(ii) details of any adverse reaction to the product so sold or supplied of which he becomes aware.

(5) The licence holder shall import no more on any one occasion than such amount as is sufficient for 25 single administrations, or for 25 courses of treatment where the amount imported is sufficient for a maximum of three months' treatment, and on any such occasion shall not import more than the quantity notified to the licensing authority under subparagraph (1)(d).

(6) The licence holder shall inform the licensing authority forthwith of any matter coming to his attention which might reasonably cause the licensing authority to believe that the medicinal product can no longer be regarded either as a product which can safely be administered to human beings or as a product which is of satisfactory quality for such administration.

(7) The licence holder shall not issue any advertisement, catalogue or circular relating to the special medicinal product or make any representations in respect of that product.

(8) The licence holder shall cease importing or supplying a special medicinal product if he has received a notice in writing from the licensing authority directing that, as from a date specified in that notice, a particular product or class of products shall no longer be imported or supplied.

The licence holder shall take all reasonable precautions and exercise all due diligence to ensure that any information he provides to the licensing authority which is relevant to an evaluation of the safety, quality or efficacy of any medicinal product for human use which he handles, stores or distributes is not false or misleading in a material particular.

Where a wholesale dealer's licence relates to exempt advanced therapy medicinal products the licence holder shall keep the data for the system for the traceability of the advanced therapy medicinal products for such period, being a period of longer than 30 years, as may be specified by the licensing authority.

The Standard Provisions also require the holder of a wholesale dealer's licence that relates to exempt advanced therapy medicinal products to obtain supplies of exempt advanced therapy medicinal products only from the holder of a manufacturer's licence in respect of those products or the holder of a wholesale dealer's licence in respect of those products.

The licence holder must:

- distribute an exempt advanced therapy medicinal product by way of wholesale dealing only to the holder of a wholesale dealer's licence in respect of those products; or a person who may lawfully administer those products, and solicited the product for an individual patient.
- establish and maintain a system ensuring that the exempt advanced therapy medicinal product and its starting and raw materials, including all substances coming into contact with the cells or tissues it may contain, can be traced through the sourcing, manufacturing, packaging, storage, transport and delivery to the establishment where the product is used.
- inform the licensing authority of any adverse reaction to any exempt advanced therapy medicinal product supplied by the holder of the wholesale dealer's licence of which the holder is aware.
- keep the data referred to in paragraph 16 for a minimum of 30 years after the expiry date of the exempt advanced therapy medicinal product.
- ensure that the data referred to in paragraph 16 will, in the event that the licence is suspended, revoked or withdrawn or the licence holder becomes bankrupt or insolvent, be held available to the licensing authority by the holder of a wholesale dealer's licence for the period described in paragraph 18 or such longer period as may be required pursuant to paragraph 44 of Schedule 4.
- not import or export any exempt advanced therapy medicinal product.

Appointment and Duties of the Responsible Person

Title VII of the Directive on the Community code relating to medicinal products for human use (Directive 2001/83/EC) obliges holders of a distribution authorisation to have a "qualified person designated as responsible". Regulation 45 of the Human Medicines Regulations 2012 [SI 2012/1916] state the requirement for a Responsible Person (RP) within the UK.

The RP is responsible for safeguarding product users against potential hazards arising from poor distribution practices as a result, for example, of purchasing suspect products, poor storage or failure to establish the bona fides of purchasers. The duties of a RP include:

- to ensure that the provisions of the licence are observed
- to ensure that the guidelines on Good Distribution Practice (GDP) are complied with
- to ensure that the operations do not compromise the quality of medicines
- to ensure that an adequate quality system is established and maintained
- to oversee audit of the quality system and to carry out independent audits
- to ensure that adequate records are maintained
- to ensure that all personnel are trained
- to ensure full and prompt cooperation with marketing authorisation holders in the event of recalls.

In order to carry out his duties, the RP should be resident in the UK have a clear reporting line to the licence holder or MD. The RP should have personal knowledge of the products traded under the licence and the conditions necessary for their safe storage and distribution. The RP should have access to all areas, sites, stores and records which relate to the licensable activities and regularly review and monitor all such areas, etc. and the standards achieved.

If the RP is not adequately carrying out those duties, the licensing authority may consider the suspension of the licence, withdrawal of acceptance of the RP on that licence and the acceptability on any other licence.

The RP does not have to be an employee of the licence holder but must be available to the licence holder when required. Where the RP is not an employee, there should be a written contract specifying responsibilities, duties, authority and so on.

In the case of small companies, the licensing authority may accept the licence holder as the nominated RP. In larger companies, however, this is not desirable.

There is no statutory requirement for the RP to be a pharmacist.

The RP should have access to pharmaceutical knowledge and advice when it is required, and have personal knowledge of:

(a) The relevant provisions of the Human Medicines Regulations 2012 [SI 2012/1916].
(b) Directive 2001/83/EC as amended on the wholesale distribution of medicinal products for human use.
(c) The EU Guidelines on Good Distribution Practice of Medicinal Products for Human Use (2013/C 68/01).
(d) The conditions of the wholesale dealer's licence for which nominated.
(e) The products traded under the licence and the conditions necessary for their safe storage and distribution.
(f) The categories of persons to whom products may be distributed.

Where the RP is not a pharmacist or eligible to act as a Qualified Person (QP) (as defined in Directive 2001/83/EC as amended), the RP should have at least one year's practical experience in both or either of the following areas:

(a) Handling, storage and distribution of medicinal products.
(b) Transactions in or selling or procuring medicinal products.

In addition, the RP should have at least one year's managerial experience in controlling and directing the wholesale distribution of medicinal products on a scale, and of a kind, appropriate to the licence for which nominated.

To carry out responsibilities, the RP should:

(a) Have a clear reporting line to either the licence holder or the Managing Director.
(b) Have access to all areas, sites, stores, staff and records relating to the licensable activities being carried out.
(c) Demonstrate regular review and monitoring of all such areas, sites and staff etc. or have delegated arrangements whereby the RP receives written reports that such delegated actions have been carried out on behalf of the RP in compliance with standard operating procedures and GDP.

Where arrangements are delegated, the RP remains responsible and should personally carry out the delegated functions at least once a year.

(d) Focus on the management of licensable activities, the accuracy and quality of records, compliance with standard operating procedures and GDP, the quality of handling and storage equipment and facilities, and the standards achieved.
(e) Keep appropriate records relating to the discharge of the RP responsibilities.

Where the licence covers a number of sites, the RP may have a nominated deputy with appropriate reporting and delegating arrangements. However, the RP should be able to demonstrate to the licensing authority that the necessary controls and checks are in place.

The licence holder should ensure that there is a written standard operating procedure for receiving advice and comment from the RP and recording the consequent action taken as may be necessary.

Should it prove impossible to resolve a disagreement between the licence holder and the RP, the licensing authority should be consulted.

Whilst a joint referral is clearly to be preferred, either party may approach the licensing authority independently. If an RP finds difficulty over performing statutory responsibilities or the activities being carried out under the licence, the licensing authority should be consulted in strict confidence.

Control and Monitoring of Storage and Transportation Temperatures

Editor's note: Legislation and good practices oblige pharmaceutical manufacturers and distributors to exercise control over the distribution chain to ensure that the quality of medicines is maintained and assured. Critical in this regard is control of the environmental conditions under which medicines are stored and transported. The MHRA's recommendations concerning the control and monitoring of storage and transportation temperatures were published in The Pharmaceutical Journal in July 2001[5]. These recommendations have been further developed in line with development of the supply chain, technologies and GDP.

Introduction

1 EU requirements and guidelines on Good Distribution Practice (GDP) require distributors to ensure that medicinal products are maintained within appropriate temperature conditions at all times including during storage and transportation. The requirements are applicable not only to medicines that need to be stored at low temperatures typically 2°C to 8°C, known as cold chain products, but also to medicines that do not require low temperature storage, typically below 25°C or 30°C, referred to as temperate chain products. In addition, an increasing number of products require storage and transportation at sub-zero temperatures and the application of appropriate controls to these is equally important. What follows gives guidance on how compliance with relevant standards of GDP may be achieved.

Why Control and Monitor Temperature?

2 Manufacturers subject their products to stability studies that are used to determine appropriate storage conditions including those for temperature. These conditions are therefore specific for each product, and wholesalers should refer to manufacturers' information when deciding the storage conditions to use.

---

[5] Taylor J. Recommendations on the control and monitoring of storage and transportation temperatures of medicinal products. *Pharm J* 2001; 267: 128–131.

Medicinal products experiencing an adverse temperature may undergo physical, chemical or microbiological degradation. In the most serious of cases this may lead to conversion of the medicine to ineffective or harmful forms. The ability to detect these changes may not appear until the medicine is consumed, and it is therefore essential that appropriate temperature conditions are controlled and monitored throughout each step of the supply chain.

Control and Monitoring of Storage Areas

3   All equipment involved in temperature control, monitoring and storage of pharmaceuticals should be demonstrated to be fit for purpose, appropriately qualified prior to use and reassessed routinely. Such equipment may include HVAC systems, temperature monitors, related computer systems, cold rooms, refrigerators and freezers. A programme of routine servicing and maintenance should ensure equipment performs as intended.

4   Where medicines are stored that may be required in an emergency then contingency measures should be put in place such as linking essential equipment in a large warehouse to a source of emergency power supply. These emergency measures should be routinely tested, such as the confirmation of restoration of stored data and settings when emergency power supply is activated and after normal power is resumed. For these products there should be a system in place to ensure that on-call personnel are notified in the event of power failure or temperature alarms being triggered including notification outside of normal working hours.

5   Where a temperature excursion is experienced such as excessive cooling, the temperature should be recorded together with time and date and the corrective action carried out and recorded. After a short period when the corrective action has taken effect the temperature and time should be recorded again and the thermometer reset. The impact of the excursion can therefore be more properly assessed.

6   The application of Mean Kinetic Temperature (MKT) to temperature monitoring of wholesale products is only appropriate where an acceptable MKT value is provided by the MA holder for a specific product, and the recording of temperature can be confirmed to be consistent and complete from the moment of leaving the manufacturer's premises. In practice the application of MKT fails where a complete chain of temperature recording cannot be allocated to a specific consignment of a product. Attempts to apply MKT have been proposed by wholesalers as an alternative to having adequate temperature control within their warehouses as well as attempting to downgrade the impact of temperature excursions. The use

of MKT in the wholesale environment without robust supporting information and methodology is therefore discouraged.

Temperature Monitoring in Temperate Storage Areas

7   The majority of medicines require storage in temperate conditions with a maximum of 25°C or 30°C. Although minimum temperatures are often not quoted for temperate products, some formulations are more susceptible to cold extremes including oils, creams, gels and syrups in which cases a suitable minimum acceptable storage temperature should be documented. The design of the warehouse and the control of product movement should enable product to be maintained in appropriate temperature conditions at all times, including when being held in receiving areas, quarantine areas and loading bays.

8   The simplest monitoring would be for a small warehouse with a maximum/ minimum thermometer placed at a strategic location with the maximum and minimum temperatures read, recorded and the thermometer reset daily. With the exception of very small stores temperatures should be recorded at positions of temperature gradient extremes such as low and high locations. Continuous temperature recording is recommended for large warehouses and self-contained storage areas within warehouses (e.g. controlled drug store, flammables store), which should be included in temperature monitoring programmes. There should be a means to identify temperature excursions or read live temperatures in addition to the ability to review temperature records over a recording period. Temperature records should be routinely reviewed for accuracy and completeness and to monitor trends.

Temperature Monitoring in Cold Chain Storage Areas

9   Many medicinal products require storage at controlled low temperature. The principles outlined for temperature control and monitoring of temperate products also apply to cold chain but need to be interpreted in the context of the cold chain environment with its narrow acceptable temperature range, specialised equipment involved and increased suscep- tibility of cold chain product to temperature extremes. Some cold chain products such as vaccines, insulin, blood products and some products of biotechnology can be denatured by freezing and thus must be maintained within a narrow temperature range above freezing point.

10 The temperature in refrigerators used to store medicines should be measured continuously by a calibrated device and the maximum and minimum temperatures recorded daily. Refrigerators used for vaccines and

other sensitive products should be capable of maintaining the temperature between 2°C and 8°C with the minimum of intervention. Temperature monitoring of these should be by an electronic maximum/minimum thermometer with an accuracy of ±0.5°C and precision of at least ±0.1°C which should be readable from outside the unit. Alarms should be fitted capable of indicating when unacceptable temperatures have been reached, should not cancel automatically and should be routinely tested. Temperature monitoring should enable readings to be made with the door shut, and where temperature probes are buffered the buffering should be representative of the most sensitive product being stored. Refrigerators should not be sited in an environment where extremes of temperature will affect their performance. This external temperature, typically in the range of <10°C or >30°C, is often documented in the manufacturers' specification for the unit.

SMALL REFRIGERATORS

11   Refrigerators used to store pharmaceuticals should be demonstrated to be fit for purpose. In the simplest of cases a new off-the–shelf refrigerator installed according to the manufacturer's instructions and temperature monitored with an appropriate device may be considered appropriately qualified for storing cold chain product that is shown to be unaffected by minor temperature excursions. A refrigerator used for holding more susceptible stock such as biological products will require more extensive qualification.

12   In addition to temperature mapping and monitoring there should be safeguards to preserve appropriate storage conditions. Some small refrigerators are purported to be medical or pharmaceutical refrigerators but this on its own does not automatically render them suitable for wholesale use. The refrigerator should be capable of restoring the temperature quickly after the door has been opened and without danger of overshooting to extreme cold. This could be assisted by an internal fan and good shelf design which enables an efficient air flow. There should be no internal ice box and no internal temperature dials capable of being inadvertently knocked and adjusted.

13   Storage practices for using small refrigerators should include consideration of segregation of stock with different status, e.g. incoming, quarantine, returned and outgoing stock. Sufficient space should be maintained to permit adequate air circulation and product should not be stored in contact with the walls or on the floor of the refrigerator. If the refrigerator is filled to capacity the effect on temperature distribution should be investigated. Where non-refrigerated items are introduced to the refrigerator, such as

non-conditioned gel packs, the impact of introducing these items should be assessed regarding the increase in temperature they cause.

14   These should be of appropriate design, suitably sited and be constructed with appropriate materials. The design should ensure general principles of GDP can be maintained, such as segregation of stock. Condensate from chillers should not be collected inside the unit and there should be a capability to carry out routine maintenance and service activities as much as possible from outside the unit. The temperature should be monitored with an electronic temperature-recording device that measures load temperature in one or more locations depending on the size of the unit, and alarms should be fitted to indicate power outages and temperature excursions.

15   Qualification documentation should be obtained from the installer to ensure the unit is installed to an appropriate standard and can operate as required. Internal air temperature distribution should be mapped on installation in the empty and full state and annually thereafter under conditions of normal use. Products should not be stored in areas shown by temperature mapping to present a risk, e.g. in the airflow from the refrigeration unit or directly on the floor.

16   The same general principles apply to freezers as apply to other cold chain storage units above. Walk-in freezers pose a significant operator health and safety risk, and the impact of ways of working should be reviewed with consideration of risk to causing temperature excursions.

Temperature Mapping

17   With rare exception, all warehouses and refrigerators should be temperature mapped prior to use to ascertain the temperature distribution within the area used for handling medicines. The mapping exercise should be repeated where conditions significantly vary, such as with seasonal variation, alteration in storage layout and changes in supply of supplemental heating or cooling. Exceptions to the requirement to temperature map include where multiple monitoring devices spread throughout a storage area provide continuous and thorough monitoring. Mapping may also not be required where temperate storage areas are deemed too small to warrant mapping e.g. of a size to store 2 or 3 totes, in which case temperature monitoring without mapping is adequate.

18   A mapping exercise should consist of a description of the mapping method, including equipment used, placement of probes, responsibilities, types of information to be recorded and method and responsibility for analysing the data. The mapping method is commonly presented as a protocol and should be approved before any data is collected. All persons involved in the exercise should have an appropriate level of experience or training. The mapping exercise should represent conditions of normal use, and in addition to normal storage areas temperature measurement points should include high and low locations, storage areas near heat sources such as skylights and near radiators, cold areas such as returned stock areas near loading lobbies, and within enclosed areas such as controlled drug stores and cupboards.

19   Mapping data should be traceable to the individual and equipment taking the record and be traceable to temperature recorder calibration status. Interpretation of results should include any deviations from the original method. If the outcome of the mapping exercise is accepted a summary report including any recommendations for action should be approved. Such recommendations may include the most suitable placement of temperature monitoring devices for routine temperature measurement, reassigning an acceptable warehouse temperature range or the identification of hot spots and cold spots not fit for storage.

20   The same principles apply to mapping of refrigerators and cold rooms as for temperate warehouses. Temperature data should be collected from areas likely to present areas of risk of temperature extremes such as near condensers or doors as well as throughout the general storage area and should represent operation of the storage area in normal use. Where a new piece of equipment is being mapped the conditions should be representative of use, including buffering to mimic stock holding and opening of the door. Where manual defrosting is carried out this should also be included in the data collection period.

Calibration of Temperature Monitoring Devices

21   In order to have confidence in temperature readings monitoring devices should be calibrated to demonstrate they have appropriate accuracy and precision. Temperate storage thermometers should be capable of reading $\pm1°C$, and cold chain devices capable of reading $\pm0.5°C$. Calibration should extend across the whole of the working range, so for a temperate storage range of 15°C to 25°C the calibration range may be 10°C to 30°C to allow the thermometer to be used in assessing temperature excursions or to be used in temperature mapping exercises. Results of the calibration exercise should be presented in a report or calibration certificate approved

by the calibrator and demonstrated to be appropriate for use by the wholesaler. The certificate should include the following details:

- Serial number of the calibrated instrument
- Serial numbers of test instruments
- Traceability to national or international calibration standards
- Calibration test method used
- ISO or equivalent registration details of calibration laboratory
- Date of calibration
- Calibration results
- Unique certificate number
- Approval of results by calibrator.

Where a temperature monitoring device reads temperature from a main monitoring unit plus a remote probe it should be clear from the calibration certificate which part of the device the calibration refers to. Calibration should be carried out annually, and where adjustments are made to the equipment as part of calibration an assessment of accuracy and precision should be made prior to adjustment in addition to following adjustment. On completion a suitable representative from the wholesaler should approve the calibration indicating its suitability for use.

Temperature Control and Monitoring During Transportation

22   The responsibility for assuring that goods are transported in conditions that will maintain appropriate temperature should be defined in a contract signed by the wholesale supplier and transporter company. This contract should include mechanisms of reporting temperature excursions. Vehicles should be of appropriate construction, temperature mapped in conditions approximating normal transport operation, and monitoring devices should be calibrated. Where systems of cooling or heating the vehicle storage area are in place these should be qualified.

23   The means of transportation and routes involved should be understood by the supplying wholesaler and this should form part of routine self inspection scope. The process used for loading, unloading and cross-docking should be assessed with regard to maintaining appropriate conditions throughout transportation. Where routes are used on a routine basis for standard cargoes these may be validated and the extent of routine monitoring adjusted accordingly. Where routes vary then temperature monitoring and verification is required.

24   Consideration should be given to the possible extremes of temperature inside uninsulated, unventilated delivery vehicles and precautions should

be taken to protect all products from heat challenge. This includes goods distributed using postal services.

25   Where medicines are transported by air they should be transported in a pressurised and heated hold. Similarly for goods travelling by ship the means of packaging should ensure temperatures are maintained throughout the voyage. The use of established freight forwarders and shippers can reduce the risk of product experiencing temperature excursions.

Transportation of Cold Chain Goods

26   The route and time of transportation, the local seasonal temperatures and the nature of the load should all be considered when arranging cold-chain distribution. For small volumes of cold-chain goods insulated containers may be used, in which case it is vital that products damaged by freezing are prevented from coming into direct contact with ice packs at sub-zero temperatures.

27   Larger volumes of cold-chain goods should be shipped in refrigerated transport, particularly if transit times may be prolonged. Temperatures within loads of products at risk from freezing should be strictly controlled and monitored with recording probes or individual temperature monitoring devices, giving consideration to the temperature gradient within the load. The temperature records for each consignment should be reviewed and there should be a procedure for implementing corrective action in the case of adverse events.

28   Distributors should ensure that consignments of cold-chain goods are clearly labelled with the required storage/transport conditions including the use of Time and Temperature Sensitive Product labels. Receivers should satisfy themselves that the goods have been transported under appropriate conditions and should place them in appropriate storage facilities as soon as possible after receipt.

29   The method of packing cold-chain goods should be chosen with consideration of the mode of transport. Stock packed for transport within a refrigerated van may not have thermal insulation whereas stock transported in non-refrigerated transport may be packed in an insulated box with ice packs. Where active or passive insulated packaging is used the method of packing and performance of the packaging should be ascertained and documented. This should be repeated for seasonal variation where packing configuration changes. Where cool packs or ice packs are used there should be a documented process describing the conditioning of the packs and a means to ensure only fully conditioned packs are used.

Verification of Bona Fides

Before commencing wholesale dealing activities with a customer or supplier (trading partners), wholesale dealers should ensure that their proposed trading partners are entitled to trade with them. Checks should demonstrate that trading partners hold the required manufacturing and wholesale dealer's authorisations.

Wholesale Dealers should request that trading partners supply a copy of their wholesale dealers authorisation or manufacturing authorisation before trading commences.

Subsequent and continuing bona fides checks can be made by checking against the Register of Wholesale Dealers on the MHRA website and by registering for Alerts whereby changes to a licence holders status, such as revocations and suspensions are notified by email.

Falsified Medicines

A "falsified medicinal product" means any medicinal product with a false representation of:

(a) its identity, including its packaging and labelling, its name or its composition (other than any unintentional quality defect) as regards any of its ingredients including excipients and the strength of those ingredients;
(b) its source, including its manufacturer, its country of manufacturing, its country of origin or its marketing authorisation holder; or
(c) its history, including the records and documents relating to the distribution channels used.

The supply of falsified medicines is a global phenomenon and one which the MHRA takes very seriously. Falsified medicines represent a threat to the legitimate UK supply chain and to patient safety. They are fraudulent and may be deliberately misrepresented with respect to identity, composition and/or source. Falsification can apply to both innovator and generic products, prescription and self-medication, as well as to traditional herbal remedies. Falsified medicines may include products with the correct ingredients but fake packaging, with the wrong ingredients, without active ingredients or with insufficient active ingredients, and may even contain harmful or poisonous substances.

The supply and distribution of medicines is tightly controlled within the European Community.

All licensed wholesalers must comply with the Community's agreed standards of good distribution practice (GDP) and there exist strict licensing and regulatory requirements in UK domestic legislation to safeguard patients against potential hazards arising from poor distribution practices: for example, purchasing suspect or falsified products, failing to establish the "bona fides" of suppliers and purchasers, inadequate record keeping, and so on.

Section 6.4 of the EU Guide to GDP is of principal importatnce to wholesale dealer. This states:

> "Wholesale distributors must immediately inform the competent authority and the marketing authorisation holder of any medicinal products they identify as falsified or suspect to be falsified[6]. A procedure should be in place to this effect. It should be recorded with all the original details and investigated.[1]
>
> Any falsified medicinal products found in the supply chain should immediately be physically segregated and stored in a dedicated area away from all other medicinal products. All relevant activities in relation to such products should be documented and records retained."

Wholesale dealers in particular should maintain a high level of vigilance against the procurement or supply of potentially falsified product. Such product may be offered for sale below the established market price so rigorous checks should be made on the bona fides of the supplier and the origin of the product. It is known that some wholesalers are themselves developing good practice strategies – such as conducting rigorous physical inspections of packs when grey market purchases are made – and this is encouraged. Any suspicious activity should be reported to:

Email: casereferrals@mhra.gsi.gov.uk
Telephone: +44 (0)20 3080 6330

To report suspected counterfeit medicines or medical devices:
Email: counterfeit@mhra.gsi.gov.uk
Website: www.mhra.gov.uk
Telephone: +44 (0)20 3080 6701

Regulatory Action

The Competent Authority will take regulatory action where breaches of legislation are identified; this may take the form of adverse licensing action e.g. make a variation to an existing licence, suspension or revocation of a licence and/or the instigation of criminal proceedings.

---

[6] Article 80(i) of Directive 2001/83/EC.

Diverted Medicines

Diversion is the term used for the fraudulent activity where medicines destined for non-EU markets re-enter the EU and are placed back on to the European market at a higher price.

The diversion of medicines involves medicinal products being offered at preferential prices and exported to specific markets (normally third countries) outside the EU. Diversion occurs when unscrupulous traders, on receipt of the medicines, re-export the products back to the EU – with the consequence that patients for whom these preferentially-priced medicines were intended, are denied access to them. Such products appearing on the EU market are then known as "diverted" from their intended market. This represents not only a corrupt diversion for profit, but such activity also poses the risk of inappropriate or unlicensed use, and the risk that the product may also be compromised due to poor storage and transportation.

As with counterfeit products, wholesale dealers in particular should maintain a high level of vigilance against the procurement or supply of potentially diverted product. Diverted products may be offered for sale below the established market value, therefore appropriate checks should be made on the bona fides of the supplier and the origin of the product should be ascertained.

Parallel Distribution

Parallel distribution embodies two fundamental principles of the European Community's founding Treaty (of Rome): the free movement of goods and Community-wide exhaustion of intellectual property rights. It is also referred to as parallel trade and also, less correctly (since the EEA[7] is a single market with no internal borders), as parallel import or export.

Parallel distribution exists in the absence of price harmonisation of pharmaceutical products within the European Union, i.e. when there are significant price differences between countries; this is the case in the European Union, where prices of medicines are not governed by free competition laws, but are generally fixed by the government.

It involves the transfer of genuine, original branded products, authorised in accordance with Community legislation, marketed in one Member State of the EEA at a lower price (the source country) to another EEA member state (the country of destination) by a parallel distributor, and placed on the market in competition with a therapeutically identical product already

---

[7] The member states of the European Union plus Iceland, Norway and Liechtenstein.

marketed there at a higher price by or under licence from the owner of the brand.

The pharmaceutical products which are distributed in this way are identical in all respects to the branded version marketed by the originator in the country into which it is imported. They are not copies; they do not vary in any respect from the original; and they are manufactured normally by the originator or by the licensee to the approved product specification. All such products require a Product Licence for Parallel Import (PLPI) which is a "piggy-back" authorisation granted by the competent regulatory authority (the MHRA in the UK), after extensive checks to ensure that the imported drug is therapeutically the same as the domestic version.

Parallel distributors operating in the UK are subject to a system of licensing and inspection, which ensures that licensed medicinal products conform to internationally agreed standards, and that those medicines are stored and distributed in compliance with the required regulatory standards. Distributors are required to hold a Wholesale Dealer's Licence, in accordance with Article 77 of Directive 2001/83/EC, as amended. The only exception is if a manufacturing authorisation includes provision for wholesale dealing. In accordance with the wholesaling authorisation, parallel distributors are obliged to follow GDP guidelines in accordance with Article 84 of the Directive, employ a Responsible Person and are subject to periodic inspection by the competent (licensing) authority.

In addition, parallel distributors in the country of destination (the receiving country) involved in repackaging or relabelling of product must employ at least one Qualified Person (QP), who has received the relevant education and training (in accordance with Article 48 of the Directive), with responsibility to ensure that a quality system is implemented and maintained. A Manufacturing (assembly) Authorisation is also required. Regular GMP inspections are undertaken at parallel assemblers and distributors (performing relabelling/repacking activities) by the Competent Authority in the Member State concerned to ensure that GMP is adhered to.

Parallel distributors are required to have effective recall procedures in place. The MHRA has systems in place to receive and investigate reports of packaging and labelling problems with medicines, including parallel traded products.

Relabelling/Repackaging

The goods should remain in their original packaging as long as possible. However, once the received product is approved for processing, relabelling may be undertaken in accordance with the national simplified marketing authorisation of the parallel-distributed product, under conditions of

GMP, i.e. exactly the same procedures as those followed by all pharmaceutical manufacturers.

This either involves replacement of the original outer carton with a brand new one or over-stickering the original outer carton, with both providing the approved label text in the language of the country of destination. In all cases, the existing package leaflet is removed and replaced by a new one originated by the parallel distributor in accordance with the simplified marketing authorisation in the language of the country of destination. In addition to the requirements of the PLPI marketing authorisation it may be necessary, as part of any repackaging specifications, for the applicant to address any trademark concerns that might arise. This may involve technical and commercial discussions between the trademark holder and the PLPI applicant.

Both the original cartons – if these are replaced – and the original leaflets must be destroyed. No handling of the actual product (e.g. open units of tablets or capsules) within its immediate packaging (e.g. blister or foil packs) should take place during replacement of the original carton and it is important to maintain the audit trail back to the origin.

As with any other pharmaceutical manufacturer, parallel distributor operators involved in relabelling and/or repackaging should be given regular training in GMP. Batch documentation should be retained for each batch.

Maintenance of the Integrity of the Supply Chain

Parallel distributors should only purchase medicinal products with marketing authorisations from authorised wholesalers or manufacturers in other EEA countries. The supplying wholesaler should make available before sale a copy of its wholesale authorisation and provide assurance that the supplies were obtained from the original manufacturer and/or an authorised wholesaler within the EEA.

Parallel distributors should also only sell or supply medicinal products with marketing authorisations to authorised wholesalers, registered pharmacies or other persons entitled to sell medicinal products to the general public. A copy of the authorisation should be requested if there is any doubt.

Continued Supply

Under Article 23a of Directive 2001/83/EC, as inserted by Article 1(22) of Directive 2004/27/EC, the marketing authorisation holder is required to notify the Competent Authority (MHRA in the UK) of the date of actual marketing of the medicinal product, taking account of the various presentations authorised, and to notify the Competent Authority if the product ceases to be placed on the market either temporarily or permanently. Except in exceptional circumstances, the notification must be made no less than two months before the interruption.

Any authorisation which within three years of granting is not placed on the market will cease to be valid. In respect of generic medicinal products, the three year period will start on the grant of the authorisation, or at the end of the period of market exclusivity or patent protection of the reference product, whichever is the later date. If a product is placed on the market after authorisation, but subsequently ceases to be available on the market in the UK for a period of three consecutive years, it will also cease to be valid. In these circumstances the MHRA will, however, when it is aware of the imminent expiry of the three year period, notify the marketing authorisation holder in advance that their marketing authorisation will cease to be valid. In exceptional circumstances, and on public health grounds, the MHRA may grant an exemption from the invalidation of the marketing authorisation after three years. Whether there are exceptional circumstances and public health grounds for an exemption will be assessed on a case by case basis. When assessing such cases, MHRA will, in particular, consider the implications for patients and public health more generally of an marketing authorisation no longer being valid.

The MHRA has received requests for advice on implications for maintaining the harmonisation of an authorisation across Member States if a presentation of a product is withdrawn from the market of the Reference Member State (RMS) and remains unavailable on that market for three years. Discussions on applying the sunset clause provision in such circumstances continue at EU level. In the meantime the MHRA will address the implications of this issue on a case by case basis.

Those provisions are implemented in the UK by Part 5 of the Human Medicines Regulations 2012.

In accordance with the MHRA's interpretation of the expression "placing on the market" when used elsewhere in the Directive, the MHRA's view is that a product is "placed on the market" at the first transaction by which the product enters the distribution chain in the UK. The marketing authorisation holder must, therefore, notify the MHRA when a product with a new marketing authorisation is first placed into the distribution chain, rather than the first date it becomes available to individual patients. The MHRA requests that you notify us of this first "placing on the market" within one calendar month. In order to ensure that a marketing authorisation continues to be valid, the marketing authorisation holder must ensure that at least one packaging presentation (e.g. bottle or blister pack) of the product, which can include own label supplies, authorised under that marketing authorisation is present on the market.

The marketing authorisation holder must report all cessations/ interruptions to the MHRA. However, the MHRA does not need to be notified of the following:

(a) normal seasonal changes in manufacturing and/or distribution schedules (such as cold and flu remedies);
(b) short-term temporary interruptions in placing on the market that will not affect normal availability to distributors.

If you are in doubt about whether or not you need to notify an interruption in supply, you should err on the side of caution and report it to the MHRA in the normal way. You must notify the MHRA if any of the presentations authorised under a single marketing authorisation cease to be placed on the market either temporarily or permanently, but, as stated above, the absence of availability of one or more presentations – as long as one presentation of the product authorised under the single marketing authorisation remains on the market – will not invalidate the marketing authorisation. Problems relating to manufacturing or assembly should also be discussed with the appropriate GMP Inspector and issues of availability of medicines relating to suspected or confirmed product defects should be directly notified to, and discussed with, the Defective Medicines Reporting Centre (Tel: 020 3080 6574).

The Department of Health (DH) also has an interest in the availability of products for supply to the NHS, and together with the Association of the British Pharmaceutical Industry (ABPI) and the British Generics Manufacturers Association (BGMA), has developed best practice guidelines for notifying medicine shortages. These guidelines, together with DH/ABPI guidelines "Ensuring Best Practice in the Notification of Product Discontinuations" complement the statutory requirements under the European legislation and may be found (in PDF format) on the DH website (www.dh.gov.uk). Marketing authorisation holders should, therefore, continue to notify the Department of Health about interruptions and cessations of marketing in accordance with these guidelines.

In this context, your attention is also drawn to Article 81 of Directive 2001/83/EC as substituted by Article 1(57) of Directive 2004/27/EC, under which the marketing authorisation holder and the distributors of a medicinal product actually placed on the market shall, within the limits of their responsibilities, ensure appropriate and continued supplies of that medicinal product to pharmacies and persons authorised to supply medicinal products so that the needs of patients in the Member State in question are covered. Failure by a marketing authorisation holder to comply with this obligation is a criminal offence, unless the marketing authorisation holder took all reasonable precautions and exercised all due diligence to avoid such a failure.

Product Recall/Withdrawal

The Human Medicines Regulations 2012 [SI 2012/1916] imposes certain obligations on licence holders with regard to withdrawal and recall from sale. The aim of the Defective Medicines Report Centre (DMRC) within the MHRA is to minimise the hazard to patients arising from the distribution of defective (human) medicinal products by providing an emergency assessment and communications system between the suppliers (manufacturers and distributors), the regulatory authorities and the end user. The DMRC achieves this by receiving reports of suspected defective (human) medicinal products; monitoring and, as far as is necessary, directing and advising actions by the relevant licence holder(s) and communicating the details of this action with the appropriate urgency and distribution to users of the products. The communication normally used is a "Drug Alert".

A defective medicinal product is one whose quality does not conform to the requirements of its marketing authorisation, specification or for some other reason of quality is potentially hazardous. A defective product may be suspected because of a visible defect or contamination or as a result of tests performed on it, or because it has caused untoward reactions in a patient or for other reasons involving poor manufacturing or distribution practice.

An adverse drug reaction means a response to a medicinal product which is noxious and unintended and which occurs at doses normally used in man for the prophylaxis, diagnosis or therapy of disease or for the restoration, correction or modification of physiological function.

Falsified medicines are considered as defective products.

Immediately a hazard is identified from any source, it will be necessary to evaluate the level of danger, and the category of recall, if required. Where the reported defect is a confirmed defect, the DMRC will then take one of the following courses of action and obtain a report from the manufacturer on the nature of the defect, their handling of the defect and action to be taken to prevent its recurrence.

Issue a "Recall"

Under normal circumstances a recall is always required where a defect is confirmed unless the defect is shown to be of a trivial nature and/or there are unlikely to be significant amounts of the affected product remaining in the market.

It is the licence holder's responsibility to recall products from customers, in a manner agreed with the DMRC. The company should provide copies of draft recall letters for agreement with the DMRC. If the company (licence holder) does not agree to a recall voluntarily, the MHRA, as Licensing Authority, may be obliged to take compulsory action.

Issue a "Drug Alert"

Recall and withdrawal of product from the market is normally the responsibility of the licence holder. However, where a product has been distributed widely and/or there is a serious risk to health from the defect, the MHRA can opt to issue a Drug Alert letter. The Drug Alert cascade mechanism ensures rapid communication of safety information; it is not a substitute for, but complementary to, any action taken by the licence holder. The text of the Alert should be agreed between the MHRA and the company concerned.

In some cases, where a product has been supplied to a small number of known customers, the MHRA may decide that notification will be adequate and a Drug Alert is not needed.

The DMRC may also request companies to insert notification in the professional press in certain cases.

Management of the Recall

The company should directly contact wholesalers, hospitals, retail pharmacies and overseas distributors supplied. The DMRC is likely to take the lead in notifying Regional Contacts for NHS Trusts and Provider Units and Health Authorities, special and Government hospitals and overseas regulatory authorities.

The DMRC will liaise with the company and discuss arrangements for the recall, requesting the dates that supply started and ceased and a copy of any letters sent out by that company concerning the recall. Again, it is desirable that the text of the notices sent via the company and by the DMRC should be mutually agreed.

Follow-up Action

The DMRC will monitor the conduct and success of the recall by the manufacturer or distributor. As follow-up action, it may be necessary to consider any or all of the following:

- arrange a visit to the licence holder/manufacturer/distributor;
- arrange a visit to the point of discovery of the defect;
- refer to the Inspectorate to arrange an inspection;
- seek special surveillance of adverse reaction reports;
- refer the matter for adverse licensing and/or enforcement action.

Reporting a Suspected Defect

Suspected defects can be reported by telephone, e-mail or letter or using our online form:

Address:
DMRC, 5th Floor Yellow Zone, 151 Buckingham Palace Road, London, SW1W 9SZ, UK.
Telephone: +44 (0)20 3080 6574 (08:45 – 16:45 Monday to Friday)
Telephone: +44 (0)7795 641532 (urgent calls outside working hours, at weekends or on public holidays)
E-mail: dmrc@mhra.gsi.gov.uk
Online form: www.mhra.gov.uk
http://www.mhra.gov.uk/Safetyinformation/Reportingsafetyproblems/Reportingsuspecteddefectsinmedicines/Suspecteddefectonlineform/index.htm

UK Guidance on Brokering Medicines

Contents

Introduction

Persons procuring, holding, storing, supplying or exporting medicinal products are required to hold a wholesale distribution authorisation in accordance with Directive 2001/83/EC which lays down the rules for the wholesale distribution of medicinal products in the Union.

However, the distribution network for medicinal products may involve operators who are not necessarily authorised wholesale distributors. To ensure the reliability of the supply chain, Directive 2011/62/EU, the Falsified Medicines Directive extends medicine legislation to the entire supply chain. This now includes not only wholesale distributors, whether or not they physically handle the medicinal products, but also brokers who are involved in the sale or purchase of medicinal products without selling or purchasing those products themselves, and without owning and physically handling the medicinal products.

Brokering in Medicinal Products

Brokering of medicinal products is defined in the Falsified Medicines Directive and means:

All activities in relation to the sale or purchase of medicinal products, except for wholesale distribution, that do not include physical handling and that consist of negotiating independently and on behalf of another legal or natural person.

To accord with the Directive brokers may only broker medicinal products that are the subject of an authorisation granted by the European Commission or a National Competent Authority.

Brokers should be established at a permanent address and have contact details in the EU and may only operate following registration of these details with the National Competent Authority. In the UK this is the MHRA. A broker must provide required details for registration which will include their name, corporate name and permanent address. They must also notify any changes without unnecessary delay. This is to ensure the brokers accurate identification, location, communication and supervision of their activities by the National Competent Authorities.

Brokers can negotiate between the manufacturer and a wholesaler, or one wholesaler and another wholesaler, or the manufacturer or wholesale dealer with a person who may lawfully sell those products by retail or may lawfully supply them in circumstances corresponding to retail sale or a person who may lawfully administer those products.

Brokers are not virtual wholesale dealers; the definition of "Brokering medicinal products" specifically excludes the activity of "wholesale dealing". Wholesale dealing and brokering of medicinal products are separate activities. Therefore wholesale dealers who wish to broker will require a separate registration, because:

- EU legislation defines wholesale distribution and brokering a medicinal product separately;
- wholesale dealer's are licensed;
- the brokering of medicinal products is subject to registration.

Registration

UK based companies that broker medicinal products and are involved in the sale or purchase of medicinal products without selling or purchasing those products themselves, and without owning and physically handling the medicinal products are considered to be brokers and will have to register with the MHRA.

In order to register in the UK, brokers will have a permanent address and contact details in the UK and will only be allowed to operate as a bona fide broker following their successful registration with the MHRA.

Application for Brokering Registration

The registration regime for UK brokers is subject to an application procedure, followed by a determination procedure completed by the MHRA. The application procedure will include:

- making an application for registration;
- assessment by the MHRA of the application;

- providing specific evidence to check bona fides;
- advising an applicant of the decision.

UK brokers may be subject to inspection at their registered premises. This will be under a risk based inspection programme. Once registered a broker's registration will be recognised by other Member States and will allow the broker to broker across the EEA. UK medicines legislation in respect of brokering will also recognise registered brokers in other EEA Member States in the same way.

The MHRA has an obligation to enter the information on a publicly accessible UK register following the determination of successful application for registration.

This publicly available UK register is required to enable National Competent Authorities in other EEA Member States to establish the bona fides and compliance of brokers established in the UK where they are involved in the sale or purchase of medicines on their territories and the UK will investigate complaints of non-compliance. Reciprocal arrangements will apply for brokers established in other Member States involved in the sale or purchase of medicines to and from the UK.

Criteria of Broker's Registration

A person may not broker a medicinal product unless that product is covered by an authorisation granted under Regulation (EC) No 726/2004 or by a competent authority of an EEA Member State and that person is validly registered as a broker with a competent authority of an EEA Member State.

A broker is not validly registered if the broker's permanent address is not entered into a register of brokers kept by a competent authority of a member State or the registration is suspended or the broker has notified the competent authority of an EEA Member State to remove them from the register.

Brokers must satisfy all the conditions of brokering and:

- have a permanent address in the UK;
- have an emergency plan which ensures effective implementation of any recall from the market ordered by the competent authorities or carried out in cooperation with the manufacturer or marketing authorisation holder for the medicinal product concerned;
- keep records either in the form of purchase/sales invoices or on computer, or in any other form, giving for any transaction in medicinal products brokered at least the following information:
  - date on which the sale or purchase of the product is brokered;
  - name of the medicinal product;

     – quantity brokered;
     – name and address of the supplier or consignee, as appropriate;
     – batch number of the medicinal products at least for products bearing the safety features referred to in point (o) of Article 54 of Directive 2001/83/EC;
- keep the records available to the competent authorities, for inspection purposes, for a period of five years;
- comply with the principles and guidelines of good distribution practice for medicinal products as laid down in Article 84 of Directive 2001/83/EC;
- maintain a quality system setting out responsibilities, processes and risk management measures in relation to their activities.

Where the address at which the plan or records necessary to comply with the provisions of brokering are kept is different from the address notified in accordance with the application, the broker must ensure that the plan or records are kept at an address in the UK and inform the licensing authority of the address at which the plan or records are kept.

The broker must provide such information as may be requested by the MHRA concerning the type and quantity of medicinal products brokered within the period specified by the MHRA.

The broker must take all reasonable precautions and exercise all due diligence to ensure that any information provided by that broker to the MHRA is not false or misleading.

For the purposes of enabling the MHRA to determine whether there are grounds for suspending, revoking or varying the registration, the broker must permit a person authorised in writing by the MHRA, on production of identification, to carry out any inspection, or to take any copies, which an inspector may carry out or take under the provisions of the Human Medicines Regulations 2012 [SI 2012/1916].

Provision of Information

Once registered, a broker will have to notify the MHRA of any changes to the details for registration which might affect compliance with the requirements of the legislation in respect of brokering without unnecessary delay. This notification will be subject to a variation procedure. Responsibility for notifying the MHRA of any changes lies with the person responsible for management of the brokering activities.

The person responsible for management of the brokering activities shall be required to submit a report which shall include:

- a declaration that the broker has in place appropriate systems to ensure compliance with the requirements for brokering;

- provide the details of the systems which it has in place to ensure such compliance.

An annual compliance report will need to be submitted in relation to any application made before 31st March 2014, the date of the application and in relation to each subsequent reporting year, by the 30th April following the end of that year. The annual compliance report will be subject to a variation procedure so that the broker can change the original details provided.

The broker must without delay notify the licensing authority of any changes to the matters in respect of which evidence has been supplied in relation to the compliance report which might affect compliance with the requirements of brokering.

The broker must immediately inform the MHRA and the marketing authorisation holder, of medicinal products they are offered which they identify as falsified or suspect to be falsified.

Good Distribution Practice

The Commission's guidelines on good distribution practice, referred to in Article 84 of Directive 2001/83/EC have been updated to include specific provisions for brokering, see Chapter 8.

Legislation on Wholesale Distribution and Brokering Medicines

8

EU Legislation on Wholesale Distribution and Brokering Medicines

Contents

DIRECTIVE 2001/83/EC, AS AMENDED, TITLE VII, WHOLESALE DISTRIBUTION AND BROKERING MEDICINES

Directive 2001/83/EC of the European Parliament and of the Council of 6 November 2001 on the Community code relating to medicinal products for human use as amended.

Title VII: Wholesale Distribution and Brokering of Medicinal Products

> **Editor's note** Title VII of this Directive is reproduced below. Title VII has been amended by Directive 2011/62/EU and Directive 2012/26/EU. A new article 85a extends the need for a Wholesale Dealer's Licence for the export of medicine to a non-EEA country and to "introduced" medicines that are imported from a non-EEA country for the purpose of export back to a non-EEA country. A new article 85b introduces measures for persons brokering medicinal products. Reference should be made to the full Directive 2001/83/EU as amended for the preamble, definitions and the general and final provisions.

Article 76

1   Without prejudice to Article 6, Member States shall take all appropriate action to ensure that only medicinal products in respect of which a marketing authorization has been granted in accordance with Community law are distributed on their territory.

2   In the case of wholesale distribution and storage, medicinal products shall be covered by a marketing authorisation granted pursuant to Regulation (EC) No. 726/2004 or by the competent authorities of a Member State in accordance with this Directive.

3   Any distributor, not being the marketing authorisation holder, who imports a medicinal product from another Member State shall notify the marketing authorisation holder and the competent authority in the Member State to which the medicinal product will be imported of his intention to import that product. In the case of medicinal products which have not been granted an authorisation pursuant to Regulation (EC) No 726/2004, the notification to the competent authority shall be without prejudice to additional procedures provided for in the legislation of that Member State and to fees payable to the competent authority for examining the notification.

4   In the case of medicinal products which have been granted an authorisation pursuant to Regulation (EC) No 726/2004, the distributor shall submit the notification in accordance with paragraph 3 of this Article to the marketing authorisation holder and the Agency. A fee shall be payable to the Agency for checking that the conditions laid down in Union legislation on medicinal products and in the marketing authorisations are observed.

Article 77

1   Member States shall take all appropriate measures to ensure that the wholesale distribution of medicinal products is subject to the possession of an authorisation to engage in activity as a wholesaler in medicinal products, stating the premises located on their territory for which it is valid.

2   Where persons authorized or entitled to supply medicinal products to the public may also, under national law, engage in wholesale business, such persons shall be subject to the authorization provided for in paragraph 1.

3   Possession of a manufacturing authorization shall include authorization to distribute by wholesale the medicinal products covered by that authorization. Possession of an authorization to engage in activity as a wholesaler in medicinal products shall not give dispensation from the obligation to possess a manufacturing authorization and to comply with the conditions set out in that respect, even where the manufacturing or import business is secondary.

4   Member States shall enter the information relating to the authorisations referred to in paragraph 1 of this Article in the Union database referred to in Article 111(6). At the request of the Commission or any Member State, Member States shall provide all appropriate information concerning the individual authorisations which they have granted under paragraph 1 of this Article.

5   Checks on the persons authorised to engage in activity as a wholesaler in medicinal products, and the inspection of their premises, shall be carried out under the responsibility of the Member State which granted the authorisation for premises located on its territory.

6   The Member State which granted the authorization referred to in paragraph 1 shall suspend or revoke that authorization if the conditions of authorization cease to be met. It shall forthwith inform the other Member States and the Commission thereof.

7   Should a Member State consider that, in respect of a person holding an authorization granted by another Member State under the terms of paragraph 1, the conditions of authorization are not, or are no longer met, it shall forthwith inform the Commission and the other Member State involved. The latter shall take the measures necessary and shall inform the Commission and the first Member State of the decisions taken and the reasons for those decisions.

Article 78

Member States shall ensure that the time taken for the procedure for examining the application for the distribution authorization does not exceed 90 days from the day on which the competent authority of the Member State concerned receives the application.

The competent authority may, if need be, require the applicant to supply all necessary information concerning the conditions of authorization. Where the authority exercises this option, the period laid down in the first paragraph shall be suspended until the requisite additional data have been supplied.

Article 79

In order to obtain the distribution authorization, applicants must fulfil the following minimum requirements:

(a) they must have suitable and adequate premises, installations and equipment, so as to ensure proper conservation and distribution of the medicinal products;

(b) they must have staff, and in particular, a qualified person designated as responsible, meeting the conditions provided for by the legislation of the Member State concerned;

(c) they must undertake to fulfil the obligations incumbent on them under the terms of Article 80.

Article 80

Holders of the distribution authorization must fulfil the following minimum requirements:

(a) they must make the premises, installations and equipment referred to in Article 79(a) accessible at all times to the persons responsible for inspecting them;

(b) they must obtain their supplies of medicinal products only from persons who are themselves in possession of the distribution authorization or who are exempt from obtaining such authorization under the terms of Article 77(3);

(c) they must supply medicinal products only to persons who are themselves in possession of the distribution authorization or who are authorized or entitled to supply medicinal products to the public in the Member State concerned;

(ca) they must verify that the medicinal products received are not falsified by checking the safety features on the outer packaging, in accordance with the requirements laid down in the delegated acts referred to in Article 54a(2);

(d) they must have an emergency plan which ensures effective implementation of any recall from the market ordered by the competent authorities or carried out in cooperation with the manufacturer or marketing authorization holder for the medicinal product concerned;

(e) they must keep records either in the form of purchase/sales invoices or on computer, or in any other form, giving for any transaction in medicinal products received, dispatched or brokered at least the following information:

- date,
- name of the medicinal product,
- quantity received, supplied or brokered,
- name and address of the supplier or consignee, as appropriate,
- batch number of the medicinal products at least for products bearing the safety features referred to in point (o) of Article 54;

(f) they must keep the records referred to under (e) available to the competent authorities, for inspection purposes, for a period of five years;

(g) they must comply with the principles and guidelines of good distribution practice for medicinal products as laid down in Article 84.

(h) they must maintain a quality system setting out responsibilities, processes and risk management measures in relation to their activities;

(i) they must immediately inform the competent authority and, where applicable, the marketing authorisation holder, of medicinal products they receive or are offered which they identify as falsified or suspect to be falsified.

For the purposes of point (b), where the medicinal product is obtained from another wholesale distributor, wholesale distribution authorisation holders must verify compliance with the principles and guidelines of good distribution practices by the supplying wholesale distributor. This includes verifying whether the supplying wholesale distributor holds a wholesale distribution authorisation.

Where the medicinal product is obtained from the manufacturer or importer, wholesale distribution authorisation holders must verify that the manufacturer or importer holds a manufacturing authorisation.

Where the medicinal product is obtained through brokering, the wholesale distribution authorisation holders must verify that the broker involved fulfils the requirements set out in this Directive.

Article 81

With regard to the supply of medicinal products to pharmacists and persons authorised or entitled to supply medicinal products to the public, Member States shall not impose upon the holder of a distribution authorisation which has been granted by another Member State any obligation, in particular public service obligations, more stringent than those they impose on persons whom they have themselves authorised to engage in equivalent activities.

The holder of a marketing authorisation for a medicinal product and the distributors of the said medicinal product actually placed on the market in a Member State shall, within the limits of their responsibilities, ensure appropriate and continued supplies of that medicinal product to pharmacies and persons authorised to supply medicinal products so that the needs of patients in the Member State in question are covered.

The arrangements for implementing this Article should, moreover, be justified on grounds of public health protection and be proportionate in relation to the objective of such protection, in compliance with the Treaty rules, particularly those concerning the free movement of goods and competition.

Article 82

For all supplies of medicinal products to a person authorized or entitled to supply medicinal products to the public in the Member State concerned, the authorized wholesaler must enclose a document that makes it possible to ascertain:

- batch number of the medicinal products at least for products bearing the safety features referred to in point (o) of Article 54;
- the date;
- the name and pharmaceutical form of the medicinal product;
- the quantity supplied;
- the name and address of the supplier and consignor.

Member States shall take all appropriate measures to ensure that persons authorized or entitled to supply medicinal products to the public are able to provide information that makes it possible to trace the distribution path of every medicinal product.

Article 83

The provisions of this Title shall not prevent the application of more stringent requirements laid down by Member States in respect of the wholesale distribution of:

- narcotic or psychotropic substances within their territory;
- medicinal products derived from blood;
- immunological medicinal products;
- radiopharmaceuticals.

Article 84

The Commission shall publish guidelines on good distribution practice. To this end, it shall consult the Committee for Medicinal Products for Human Use and the Pharmaceutical Committee established by Council Decision 75/320/EEC.[1]

Article 85

This Title shall apply to homeopathic medicinal products.

Article 85a

In the case of wholesale distribution of medicinal products to third countries, Article 76 and point (c) of the first paragraph of Article 80 shall not apply. Moreover, points (b) and (ca) of the first paragraph of Article 80 shall not apply where a product is directly received from a third country but not imported. However, in that case wholesale distributors shall ensure that the medicinal products are obtained only from persons who are authorised or entitled to supply medicinal products in accordance with the applicable legal and administrative provisions of the third country concerned. Where wholesale distributors supply medicinal products to persons in third countries, they shall ensure that such supplies are only made to persons who are authorised or entitled to receive medicinal products for wholesale distribution or supply to the public in accordance with the applicable legal and administrative provisions of the third country concerned. The requirements set out in Article 82 shall apply to the supply of medicinal products to persons in third countries authorised or entitled to supply medicinal products to the public.

---

[1] OJ L 147, 9.6.1975, p. 23.

Article 85b

1   Persons brokering medicinal products shall ensure that the brokered medicinal products are covered by a marketing authorisation granted pursuant to Regulation (EC) No 726/2004 or by the competent authorities of a Member State in accordance with this Directive.

Persons brokering medicinal products shall have a permanent address and contact details in the Union, so as to ensure accurate identification, location, communication and supervision of their activities by competent authorities.

The requirements set out in points (d) to (i) of Article 80 shall apply *mutatis mutandis* to the brokering of medicinal products.

2   Persons may only broker medicinal products if they are registered with the competent authority of the Member State of their permanent address referred to in paragraph 1. Those persons shall submit, at least, their name, corporate name and permanent address in order to register. They shall notify the competent authority of any changes thereof without unnecessary delay.

Persons brokering medicinal products who had commenced their activity before 2 January 2013 shall register with the competent authority by 2 March 2013.

The competent authority shall enter the information referred to in the first subparagraph in a register that shall be publicly accessible.

3   The guidelines referred to in Article 84 shall include specific provisions for brokering.

4   This Article shall be without prejudice to Article 111. Inspections referred to in Article 111 shall be carried out under the responsibility of the Member State where the person brokering medicinal products is registered.

If a person brokering medicinal products does not comply with the requirements set out in this Article, the competent authority may decide to remove that person from the register referred to in paragraph 2. The competent authority shall notify that person thereof.

9

UK Legislation on Wholesale Distribution

Contents

The Human Medicines Regulations 2012 [SI 2012/1916]

> Editor's note   These extracts from the Regulations and Standard Provisions of the Human Medicines Regulations 2012 [SI 2012/1916] are presented for the reader's convenience. Reproduction is with the permission of HMSO and the Queen's Printer for Scotland. For any definitive information reference must be made to the original Regulations. The numbering and content within this section corresponds with the regulations set out in the published Statutory Instrument (SI 2012 No.1916).

Citation and Commencement

1   (1)   These Regulations may be cited as the Human Medicines Regulations 2012.

(2)   These Regulations come into force on 14th August 2012.

General Interpretation

8   (1)   In these Regulations (unless the context otherwise requires):

"the 2001 Directive" means Directive 2001/83/EC of the European Parliament and of the Council on the Community Code relating to medicinal products for human use;

"Article 126a authorisation" means an authorisation granted by the licensing authority under Part 8 of these Regulations;

"brokering" means all activities in relation to the sale or purchase of medicinal products, except for wholesale distribution, that do not include physical handling and that consist of negotiating independently and on behalf of another legal or natural person;

"Directive 2002/98/EC" means Directive 2002/98/EC of the European Parliament and of the Council of 27 January 2003 setting standards of quality and safety for the collection, testing, processing, storage and distribution of human blood and blood components and amending Directive 2001/83/EC;

"Directive 2004/23/EC" means Directive 2004/23/EC of the European Parliament and of the Council of 31 March 2004 on setting standards of quality and safety for the donation, procurement, testing, processing, preservation, storage and distribution of human tissues and cells;

"electronic communication" means a communication transmitted (whether from one person to another, from one device to another or from a person to a device or vice versa):

(a) by means of an electronic communications network within the meaning of section 32(1) of the Communications Act 2003; or

(b) by other means but while in an electronic form;

"EU marketing authorisation" means a marketing authorisation granted or renewed by the European Commission under Regulation (EC) No 726/2004;

"European Economic Area" or "EEA" means the European Economic Area created by the EEA agreement;

"exempt advanced therapy medicinal product" has the meaning given in regulation 171;

"export" means export, or attempt to export, from the United Kingdom, whether by land, sea or air;

"falsified medicinal product" means any medicinal product with a false representation of:

(a) its identity, including its packaging and labelling, its name or its composition (other than any unintentional quality defect) as regards any of its ingredients including excipients and the strength of those ingredients;

(b) its source, including its manufacturer, its country of manufacturing, its country of origin or its marketing authorisation holder; or

(c) its history, including the records and documents relating to the distribution channels used;

"Fees Regulations" means the Medicines (Products for Human Use) (Fees) Regulations 2013[1];

"herbal medicinal product" means a medicinal product whose only active ingredients are herbal substances or herbal preparations (or both);

"herbal preparation" means a preparation obtained by subjecting herbal substances to processes such as extraction, distillation, expression, fractionation, purification, concentration or fermentation, and includes a comminuted or powdered herbal substance, a tincture, an extract, an essential oil, an expressed juice or a processed exudate;

"herbal substance" means a plant or part of a plant, algae, fungi or lichen, or an unprocessed exudate of a plant, defined by the plant part used and the botanical name of the plant, either fresh or dried, but otherwise unprocessed;

"homoeopathic medicinal product" means a medicinal product prepared from homoeopathic stocks in accordance with a homoeopathic manufacturing procedure described by:

(a) the European Pharmacopoeia; or

(b) in the absence of such a description in the European Pharmacopoeia, in any pharmacopoeia used officially in an EEA State;

"import" means import, or attempt to import, into the United Kingdom, whether by land, sea or air;

"inspector" means a person authorised in writing by an enforcement authority for the purposes of Part 16 (enforcement) (and references to "the enforcement authority", in relation to an inspector, are to the enforcement authority by whom the inspector is so authorised);

"the licensing authority" has the meaning given by regulation 6(2);

"manufacturer's licence" has the meaning given by regulation 17(1);

"marketing authorisation" means:

(a) a UK marketing authorisation; or

(b) an EU marketing authorisation;

"medicinal product subject to general sale" has the meaning given in regulation 5(1) (classification of medicinal products);

---

[1] S.I. 2013/532.

"Regulation (EC) No 726/2004" means Regulation (EC) No 726/2004 of the European Parliament and of the Council of 31 March 2004 laying down Community procedures for the authorisation and supervision of medicinal products for human and veterinary use and establishing a European Medicines Agency;

"Regulation (EC) No 1394/2007" means Regulation (EC) No 1394/2007 of the European Parliament and of the Council of 13 November 2007 on advanced therapy medicinal products and amending Directive 2001/83/EC and Regulation (EC) No 726/2004;

"Regulation (EC) No 1234/2008" means Commission Regulation (EC) No 1234/2008 of 24 November 2008 concerning the examination of variations to the terms of marketing authorisations for medicinal products for human use and veterinary medicinal products;

"the relevant EU provisions" means the provisions of legislation of the European Union relating to medicinal products for human use, except to the extent that any other enactment provides for any function in relation to any such provision to be exercised otherwise than by the licensing authority;

"relevant European State" means an EEA State or Switzerland;

"relevant medicinal product" has the meaning given by regulation 48;

"special medicinal product" means a product within the meaning of regulation 167 or any equivalent legislation in an EEA State other than the United Kingdom;

"third country" means a country or territory outside the EEA:

"traditional herbal medicinal product" means a herbal medicinal product to which regulation 125 applies;

"traditional herbal registration" means a traditional herbal registration granted by the licensing authority under these Regulations;

"UK marketing authorisation" means a marketing authorisation granted by the licensing authority under:

(a) Part 5 of these Regulations; or

(b) Chapter 4 of Title III to the 2001 Directive (mutual recognition and decentralised procedure);

"wholesale dealer's licence" has the meaning given by regulation 18(1).

(2) In these Regulations, references to distribution of a product by way of wholesale dealing are to be construed in accordance with regulation 18(7) and (8).

(3) In these Regulations, references to selling by retail, or to retail sale, are references to selling a product to a person who buys it otherwise than for a purpose specified in regulation 18(8).

(4) In these Regulations, references to supplying anything in circumstances corresponding to retail sale are references to supplying it,

otherwise than by way of sale, to a person who receives it otherwise than for a purpose specified in regulation 18(8);

Conditions for Wholesale Dealer's Licence

42 (1) Regulations 43 to 45 apply to the holder of a wholesale dealer's licence (referred to in those regulations as "the licence holder") and have effect as if they were provisions of the licence (but the provisions specified in paragraph (2) do not apply to the holder of a wholesale dealer's licence insofar as the licence relates to exempt advanced therapy medicinal products).

(2) Those provisions are regulations 43(2) and (8) and 44.

(3) The requirements in Part 2 of Schedule 6 apply to the holder of a wholesale dealer's licence insofar as the licence relates to exempt advanced therapy medicinal products, and have effect as if they were provisions of the licence.

Obligations of Licence Holder

43 (1) The licence holder must comply with the guidelines on good distribution practice published by the European Commission in accordance with Article 84 of the 2001 Directive.

(2) The licence holder must ensure, within the limits of the holder's responsibility, the continued supply of medicinal products to pharmacies, and other persons who may lawfully sell medicinal products by retail or supply them in circumstances corresponding to retail sale, so that the needs of patients in the United Kingdom are met.

(3) The licence holder must provide and maintain such staff, premises, equipment and facilities for the handling, storage and distribution of medicinal products under the licence as are necessary:
(a) to maintain the quality of the products; and
(b) to ensure their proper distribution.

(4) The licence holder must inform the licensing authority of any proposed structural alteration to, or discontinuance of use of, premises to which the licence relates or which have otherwise been approved by the licensing authority.

(5) Subject to paragraph (6), the licence holder must not sell or supply a medicinal product, or offer it for sale or supply, unless:
(a) there is a marketing authorisation, Article 126a authorisation, certificate of registration or traditional herbal registration (an "authorisation") in force in relation to the product; and

(b) the sale or supply, or offer for sale or supply, is in accordance with the authorisation.

(6) The restriction in paragraph (5) does not apply to:

(a) the sale or supply, or offer for sale or supply, of a special medicinal product;

(b) the export to an EEA State, or supply for the purposes of such export, of a medicinal product which may be placed on the market in that State without a marketing authorisation, Article 126a authorisation, certificate of registration or traditional herbal registration by virtue of legislation adopted by that State under Article 5(1) of the 2001 Directive; or

(c) the sale or supply, or offer for sale or supply, of an unauthorised medicinal product where the Secretary of State has temporarily authorised the distribution of the product under regulation 174.

(7) The licence holder must:

(a) keep documents relating to the sale or supply of medicinal products under the licence which may facilitate the withdrawal or recall from sale of medicinal products in accordance with paragraph (b);

(b) maintain an emergency plan to ensure effective implementation of the recall from the market of a medicinal product where recall is:

(i) ordered by the licensing authority or by the competent authority of any EEA State, or

(ii) carried out in co-operation with the manufacturer of, or the holder of the marketing authorisation, Article 126a authorisation, certificate of registration or traditional herbal registration for, the product; and

(c) keep records in relation to the receipt, dispatch or brokering of medicinal products, of:

(i) the date of receipt,

(ii) the date of despatch,

(iii) the date of brokering,

(iv) the name of the medicinal product,

(v) the quantity of the product received, dispatched or brokered,

(vi) the name and address of the person from whom the products were received or to whom they are dispatched,

(vii) the batch number of medicinal products bearing safety features referred to in point (o) of Article 54[2] of the 2001 Directive.

(8) A licence holder ("L") who imports from another EEA State a medicinal product in relation to which L is not the holder of a

---

[2] Point (o) of Article 54a was inserted by Directive 2011/62/EU of the European Parliament and of the Council (OJ No L 174, 1.7.2011, p74).

marketing authorisation, Article 126a authorisation, certificate of registration or a traditional herbal registration shall:

(a) notify the intention to import that product to the holder of the authorisation and:

    (i)   in the case of a product which has been granted a marketing authorisation under Regulation (EC) No 726/2004, to the EMA; or

    (ii)   in any other case, the licensing authority; and

(b) pay a fee to the EMA in accordance with Article 76(4)[3] of the 2001 Directive or the licensing authority as the case may be, in accordance with the Fees Regulations, but this paragraph does not apply in relation to the wholesale distribution of medicinal products to a person in a third country.

(9) For the purposes of enabling the licensing authority to determine whether there are grounds for suspending, revoking or varying the licence, the licence holder must permit a person authorised in writing by the licensing authority, on production of identification, to carry out any inspection, or to take any samples or copies, which an inspector could carry out or take under Part 16 (enforcement).

(10) The holder ("L") must verify in accordance with paragraph (11) that any medicinal products received by L that are required by Article 54a[4] of the Directive to bear safety features are not falsified but this paragraph does not apply in relation to the distribution of medicinal products received from a third country by a person to a person in a third country.

(11) Verification under this paragraph is carried out by checking the safety features on the outer packaging, in accordance with the requirements laid down in the delegated acts adopted under Article 54a(2) of the 2001 Directive.

(12) The licence holder must maintain a quality system setting out responsibilities, processes and risk management measures in relation to their activities.

(13) The licence holder must immediately inform the licensing authority and, where applicable, the marketing authorisation holder, of medicinal products which the licence holder receives or is offered which the licence holder:

(a) knows or suspects; or

(b) has reasonable grounds for knowing or suspecting, to be falsified.

UK LEGISLATION ON WHOLESALE DISTRIBUTION

---

[3] Article 76(4) was inserted by Directive 2011/62/EU of the European Parliament and of the Council (OJ No L 174, 1.7.2011, p74).

[4] Article 54a was inserted by Directive 2011/62/EU of the European Parliament and of the Council (OJ No L 174, 1.7.2011, p74).

(14) Where the medicinal product is obtained through brokering, the licence holder must verify that the broker involved fulfils the requirements set out in regulation 45A(1)(b).

(15) In this regulation, "marketing authorisation" means:

(a) a marketing authorisation issued by a competent authority in accordance with the 2001 Directive; or

(b) an EU marketing authorisation.

Requirement that Wholesale Dealers to Deal only with Specified Persons

44   (1) Unless paragraph (2) applies, the licence holder must not obtain supplies of medicinal products from anyone except:

(a) the holder of a manufacturer's licence or wholesale dealer's licence in relation to products of that description;

(b) the person who holds an authorisation granted by another EEA State authorising the manufacture of products of the description or their distribution by way of wholesale dealing; or

(c) where the supplier is not the holder of a manufacturer's licence, where the supply is in accordance with the principles and guidelines of good distribution practice,

but this paragraph does not apply in relation to the distribution of medicinal products directly received from a third country but not imported into the EU.

(2) From 28th October 2013 the licence holder must not obtain supplies of medicinal products from anyone except:

(a) the holder of a manufacturer's licence or wholesale dealer's licence in relation to products of that description;

(b) the person who holds an authorisation granted by another EEA State authorising the manufacture of products of the description or their distribution by way of wholesale dealing;

(c) where the medicinal product is directly received from a third country ("A") for export to a third country ("B"), the supplier of the medicinal product in country A is a person who is authorised or entitled to supply such medicinal products in accordance with the legal and administrative provisions in country A; or

(d) where the supplier is not the holder of a manufacturer's licence, where the supply is in accordance with the principles and guidelines of good distribution practice.

(3) Where a medicinal product is obtained in accordance with paragraph (1), (2)(a) or (b), the licence holder must verify that:

(a) the wholesale dealer who supplies the product complies with the principles and guidelines of good distribution practices; or

(b) the manufacturer or importer who supplies the product holds a manufacturing authorisation.

(4) Unless paragraph (5) applies, the licence holder may distribute medicinal products by way of wholesale dealing only to:

(a) the holder of a wholesale dealer's licence relating to those products;

(b) the holder of an authorisation granted by the competent authority of another EEA State authorising the supply of those products by way of wholesale dealing;

(c) a person who may lawfully sell those products by retail or may lawfully supply them in circumstances corresponding to retail sale; or

(d) a person who may lawfully administer those products,

but this paragraph does not apply in relation to medicinal products which are distributed by way of wholesale dealing to a person in a third country.

(5) From 28th October 2013, the licence holder may distribute medicinal products by way of wholesale dealing only to:

(a) the holder of a wholesale dealer's licence relating to those products;

(b) the holder of an authorisation granted by the competent authority of another EEA State authorising the supply of those products by way of wholesale dealing;

(c) a person who may lawfully sell those products by retail or may lawfully supply them in circumstances corresponding to retail sale;

(d) a person who may lawfully administer those products; or

(e) in relation to supply to persons in third countries, a person who is authorised or entitled to receive medicinal products for wholesale distribution or supply to the public in accordance with the applicable legal and administrative provisions of the third country concerned.

(6) Where a medicinal product is supplied to a person who is authorised or entitled to supply medicinal products to the public in accordance with paragraph (4)(c), (5)(c) or (e), the licence holder must enclose with the product a document stating the:

(a) date on which the supply took place;

(b) name and pharmaceutical form of the product supplied;

(c) quantity of product supplied;

(d) name and address of the licence holder; and

(e) batch number of the medicinal products bearing the safety features referred to in point (o) of Article 54 of the 2001 Directive.

(7) The licence holder must:
- (a) keep a record of information supplied in accordance with paragraph (6) for at least five years beginning immediately after the date on which the information is supplied; and
- (b) ensure that the record is available to the licensing authority for inspection.

Requirement as to Responsible Persons

45 (1) The licence holder must ensure that there is available at all times at least one person (referred to in this regulation as the "responsible person") who in the opinion of the licensing authority:
- (a) has knowledge of the activities to be carried out and of the procedures to be performed under the licence which is adequate to carry out the functions mentioned in paragraph (2); and
- (b) has adequate experience relating to those activities and procedures.

(2) Those functions are:
- (a) ensuring that the conditions under which the licence was granted have been, and are being, complied with; and
- (b) ensuring that the quality of medicinal products handled by the licence holder is being maintained in accordance with the requirements of the marketing authorisations, Article 126a authorisations, certificates of registration or traditional herbal registrations applicable to those products.

(3) The licence holder must notify the licensing authority of:
- (a) any change to the responsible person; and
- (b) the name, address, qualifications and experience of the responsible person.

(4) The licence holder must not permit any person to act as a responsible person other than the person named in the licence or another person notified to the licensing authority under paragraph (3).

(5) Paragraph (6) applies if, after giving the licence holder and a person acting as a responsible person the opportunity to make representations (orally or in writing), the licensing authority thinks that the person:
- (a) does not satisfy the requirements of paragraph (1) in relation to qualifications or experience; or
- (b) is failing to carry out the functions referred to in paragraph (2) adequately or at all.

(6) Where this paragraph applies, the licensing authority must notify the licence holder in writing that the person is not permitted to act as a responsible person.

Standard Provisions of Licences

24 (1) The standard provisions set out in Schedule 4 may be incorporated by the licensing authority in a licence under this Part granted on or after the date on which these Regulations come into force.

(2) The standard provisions may be incorporated in a licence with or without modifications and either generally or in relation to medicinal products of a particular class.

Schedule 4 Standard Provisions of Licences

PART 4 WHOLESALE DEALER'S LICENCE

All wholesale dealer's licences

28 The provisions of this Part are standard provisions of a wholesale dealer's licence.

29 The licence holder must not use any premises for the handling, storage or distribution of medicinal products other than those specified in the licence or notified to the licensing authority from time to time and approved by the licensing authority.

30 The licence holder must provide such information as may be requested by the licensing authority concerning the type and quantity of medicinal products which the licence holder handles, stores or distributes.

31 The licence holder must take all reasonable precautions and exercise all due diligence to ensure that any information provided by the licence holder to the licensing authority which is relevant to an evaluation of the safety, quality or efficacy of a medicinal product which the licence holder handles, stores or distributes is not false or misleading.

Wholesale dealer's licence relating to special medicinal products

32 The provisions of paragraphs 33 to 42 are incorporated as additional standard provisions of a wholesale dealer's licence relating to special medicinal products.

33 Where and in so far as the licence relates to special medicinal products, the licence holder may only import such products from another EEA State:

(a) in response to an order which satisfies the requirements of regulation 167, and

(b) where the conditions set out in paragraphs 34 to 41 are complied with.

UK LEGISLATION ON WHOLESALE DISTRIBUTION

34   No later than 28 days prior to each importation of a special medicinal product, the licence holder must give written notice to the licensing authority stating the intention to import the product and stating the following particulars:

(a) the brand name, common name or scientific name of the medicinal product and (if different) any name under which the medicinal product is to be sold or supplied in the United Kingdom;

(b) any trademark or the name of the manufacturer of the medicinal product;

(c) in respect of each active constituent of the medicinal product, any international non-proprietary name or the British approved name or the monograph name, or where that constituent does not have any of those, the accepted scientific name or any other name descriptive of the true nature of the constituent;

(d) the quantity of medicinal product to be imported, which must not exceed the quantity specified in paragraph 38; and

(e) the name and address of the manufacturer or assembler of the medicinal product in the form in which it is to be imported and, if the person who will supply the medicinal product for importation is not the manufacturer or assembler, the name and address of the supplier.

35   The licence holder may not import the special medicinal product if, before the end of 28 days beginning immediately after the date on which the licensing authority sends or gives the licence holder an acknowledgement in writing by the licensing authority that it has received the notice referred to in paragraph 34, the licensing authority has notified the licence holder in writing that the product should not be imported.

36   The licence holder may import the special medicinal product referred to in the notice where the licence holder has been notified in writing by the licensing authority, before the end of the 28-day period referred to in paragraph 35, that the product may be imported.

37   Where the licence holder sells or supplies special medicinal products, the licence holder must, in addition to any other records which are required by the provisions of the licence, make and maintain written records relating to:

(a) the batch number of the batch of the product from which the sale or supply was made; and

(b) details of any adverse reaction to the product sold or supplied of which the licence holder becomes aware.

38   The licence holder must not, on any one occasion, import more than such amount as is sufficient for 25 single administrations, or for 25 courses of

treatment where the amount imported is sufficient for a maximum of three months' treatment, and must not, on any one occasion, import more than the quantity notified to the licensing authority under paragraph 34(d).

39 The licence holder must inform the licensing authority immediately of any matter coming to the licence holder's attention which might reasonably cause the licensing authority to believe that a special medicinal product imported in accordance with this paragraph can no longer be regarded as a product which can safely be administered to human beings or as a product which is of satisfactory quality for such administration.

40 The licence holder must not publish any advertisement, catalogue, or circular relating to a special medicinal product or make any represen-tations in respect of that product.

41 The licence holder must cease importing or supplying a special medicinal product if the licence holder receives a notice in writing from the licensing authority directing that, from a date specified in the notice, a particular product or class of products may no longer be imported or supplied.

42 In this Part:

"British approved name" means the name which appears in the current edition of the list prepared by the British Pharmacopoeia Commission under regulation 318 (British Pharmacopoeia- lists of names);

"international non-proprietary name" means a name which has been selected by the World Health Organisation as a recommended international non-proprietary name and in respect of which the Director-General of the World Health Organisation has given notice to that effect in the World Health Organisation Chronicle; and

"monograph name" means the name or approved synonym which appears at the head of a monograph in the current edition of the British Pharmacopoeia, the European Pharmacopoeia or a foreign or international compendium of standards, and "current" in this definition means current at the time the notice is sent to the licensing authority.

Wholesale dealer's licence relating to exempt advanced therapy medicinal products

43 The provisions of paragraph 44 are incorporated as additional standard provisions of a wholesale dealer's licence relating to exempt advanced therapy medicinal products.

44 The licence holder shall keep the data referred to in paragraph 16 of Schedule 6 for such period, being a period of longer than 30 years, as may be specified by the licensing authority.

Schedule 6 Manufacturer's and Wholesale Dealer's Licences for Exempt Advanced Therapy Medicinal Products

PART 2 WHOLESALE DEALER'S LICENCES

13 The requirements in paragraphs 14 to 20 apply to a wholesale dealer's licence insofar as it relates to exempt advanced therapy medicinal products.

14 The licence holder must obtain supplies of exempt advanced therapy medicinal products only from:

(a) the holder of a manufacturer's licence in respect of those products; or
(b) the holder of a wholesale dealer's licence in respect of those products.

15 The licence holder must distribute an exempt advanced therapy medicinal product by way of wholesale dealing only to:

(a) the holder of a wholesale dealer's licence in respect of those products; or
(b) a person who:
(i)   may lawfully administer those products, and
(ii) solicited the product for an individual patient.

16 The licence holder must establish and maintain a system ensuring that the exempt advanced therapy medicinal product and its starting and raw materials, including all substances coming into contact with the cells or tissues it may contain, can be traced through the sourcing, manufacturing, packaging, storage, transport and delivery to the establishment where the product is used.

17 The licence holder must inform the licensing authority of any adverse reaction to any exempt advanced therapy medicinal product supplied by the holder of the wholesale dealer's licence of which the holder is aware.

18 The licence holder must, subject to paragraph 44 of Schedule 4, keep the data referred to in paragraph 16 for a minimum of 30 years after the expiry date of the exempt advanced therapy medicinal product.

19 The licence holder must secure that the data referred to in paragraph 16 will, in the event that:

(a) the licence is suspended, revoked or withdrawn; or
(b) the licence holder becomes bankrupt or insolvent,

be held available to the licensing authority by the holder of a wholesale dealer's licence for the period described in paragraph 18 or such longer period as may be required pursuant to paragraph 44 of Schedule 4.

20   The licence holder must not import or export any exempt advanced therapy medicinal product.

10

UK Legislation on Brokering Medicines

Contents

The Human Medicines Regulations 2012 [SI 2012/1916]

> **Editor's note** These extracts from the Human Medicines Regulations 2012 [SI 2012/1916] as amended by the Human Medicines (Amendment) Regulations 2013 [SI 2013/1855] are presented for the reader's convenience. Reproduction is with the permission of HMSO and the Queen's Printer for Scotland. For any definitive information reference must be made to the original amending Regulations. The numbering and content within this section corresponds with the regulations set out in the published Statutory Instrument (SI 2012 No. 1916) as amended.

Citation and Commencement

1 (1) These Regulations may be cited as the Human Medicines Regulations 2012.

(2) These Regulations come into force on 14th August 2012.

General Interpretation

8 (1) In these Regulations (unless the context otherwise requires)-
"brokering" means all activities in relation to the sale or purchase of medicinal products, except for wholesale distribution, that do not

include physical handling and that consist of negotiating independently and on behalf of another legal or natural person;

"falsified medicinal product" means any medicinal product with a false representation of:

(a) its identity, including its packaging and labelling, its name or its composition (other than any unintentional quality defect) as regards any of its ingredients including excipients and the strength of those ingredients;

(b) its source, including its manufacturer, its country of manufacturing, its country of origin or its marketing authorisation holder; or

(c) its history, including the records and documents relating to the distribution channels used.

Brokering in Medicinal Products

45A. (1) A person may not broker a medicinal product unless:

(a) that product is covered by an authorisation granted:

(i)   under Regulation (EC) No 726/2004; or

(ii) by a competent authority of a member State; and

(b) that person:

(i)   is validly registered as a broker with a competent authority of a member State,

(ii) except where the person is validly registered with the competent authority of another EEA state, has a permanent address in the United Kingdom, and

(iii) complies with the guidelines on good distribution practice published by the European Commission in accordance with Article 84 of the 2001 Directive insofar as those guidelines apply to brokers.

(2) A person is not validly registered for the purpose of paragraph (1)(b) if:

(a) the person's permanent address is not entered into a register of brokers kept by a competent authority of a member State;

(b) the registration is suspended; or

(c) the person has notified the competent authority of a member State to remove that person from the register.

(3) Paragraph (1)(b)(i) does not apply until 20th October 2013 in relation to a person who brokered any medicinal product before 20th August 2013.

Application for Brokering Registration

45B. (1) The licensing authority may not register a person as a broker unless paragraphs (2) to (7) are complied with.

(2) An application for registration must be made containing:
   (a) the name of the person to be registered;
   (b) the name under which that person is trading (if different to the name of that person);
   (c) that person's:
      (i) permanent address in the United Kingdom,
      (ii) e-mail address, and
      (iii) telephone number;
   (d) a statement of whether the medicinal products to be brokered are:
      (i) prescription only medicines,
      (ii) pharmacy medicines, or
      (iii) medicines subject to general sale;
   (e) an indication of the range of medicinal products to be brokered;
   (f) evidence that that person can comply with regulations 45A(1)(b)(iii), 45E(3)(a) to (f) and 45F(1); and
   (g) any fee payable in connection with the application in accordance with the Fees Regulations.

(3) Where the address at which the emergency plan, documents or record necessary to comply with regulation 45E(3)(b) to (d) are kept is different from the address notified in accordance with sub-paragraph (2)(c)(i), the application must contain:
   (a) that address where the plan or records are to be kept;
   (b) the name of a person who can provide access to that address for the purpose of regulation 325 (rights of entry); and
   (c) that person's:
      (i) address,
      (ii) e-mail address, and
      (iii) telephone number.

(4) Unless paragraph (6) applies, the application for registration must:
   (a) be in English; and
   (b) be signed by the person seeking a brokering registration.

(5) The pages of the application must be serially numbered.

(6) Where the application is made on behalf of the person seeking a brokering registration by another person ("A"), the application must:
   (a) contain the name and address of A; and
   (b) be signed by A.

Criteria of Broker's Registration

45E.   (1) Registration of a broker is conditional on that broker:
     (a) complying with regulation 45A(1); and
     (b) satisfying:
        (i) the criteria in paragraphs (3), (4) and (7), and
        (ii) such other criteria as the licensing authority considers appropriate and notifies the broker of.
    (2) The criteria referred to in paragraph (1)(b)(ii) may include (but are not limited to) the criteria specified in paragraphs (5) and (6).
    (3) The broker must:
     (a) have a permanent address in the United Kingdom;
     (b) maintain an emergency plan to ensure effective implementation of the recall from the market of a medicinal product where recall is:
        (i) ordered by the licensing authority or by the competent authority of any EEA State, or
        (ii) carried out in co-operation with the manufacturer of, or the holder of the marketing authorisation, for the product;
     (c) keep documents relating to the sale or supply of medicinal products under the licence which may facilitate the withdrawal or recall from sale of medicinal products in accordance with sub-paragraph (b);
     (d) record in relation to the brokering of each medicinal product:
        (i)   the name of the medicinal product,
        (ii) the quantity of the product brokered,
        (iii) the batch number of the medicinal product bearing the safety features referred to in point (o) of Article 54 of the 2001 Directive,
        (iv) the name and address of the:
           (aa) supplier, or
           (bb) consignee, and
        (v)   the date on which the sale or purchase of the product is brokered;
     (e) maintain a quality system setting out responsibilities, processes and risk management measures in relation to their activities; and
     (f) keep the documents or record required by sub-paragraph (c) or (d) available to the licensing authority for a period of five years; and
     (g) comply with regulation 45F(1), (2) and (4).
    (4) Where the address at which the plan or records necessary to comply with paragraph (3)(b) to (d) are kept is different from the address notified in accordance with regulation 45B(2)(c)(i), the broker must:
     (a) ensure that the plan or records are kept at an address in the United Kingdom; and
     (b) inform the licensing authority of the address at which the plan or records are kept.

(5) The broker must provide such information as may be requested by the licensing authority concerning the type and quantity of medicinal products brokered within the period specified by the licensing authority.

(6) The broker must take all reasonable precautions and exercise all due diligence to ensure that any information provided by that broker to the licensing authority in accordance with regulation 45F is not false or misleading.

(7) For the purposes of enabling the licensing authority to determine whether there are grounds for suspending, revoking or varying the registration, the broker must permit a person authorised in writing by the licensing authority, on production of identification, to carry out any inspection, or to take any copies, which an inspector may carry out or take under regulations 325 (rights of entry) and 327 (powers of inspection, sampling and seizure).

Provision of Information

45F. (1) A broker registered in the UK must immediately inform:
(a) the licensing authority; and
(b) where applicable, the marketing authorisation holder, of medicinal products which the broker identifies as, suspects to be, or has reasonable grounds for knowing or suspecting to be, falsified.

(2) On or before the date specified in paragraph (3), a broker who is, or has applied to the licensing authority to become, a registered broker in the United Kingdom must submit a report to the licensing authority, which:
(a) includes a declaration that the broker has in place an appropriate system to ensure compliance with regulations 45A, 45B and this regulation; and
(b) details the system which the broker has in place to ensure such compliance.

(3) The date specified for the purposes of this paragraph is:
(a) in relation to any application made before 31st March 2014, the date of the application; and
(b) in relation to each subsequent reporting year, 30th April following the end of that year.

(4) The broker must without delay notify the licensing authority of any changes to the matters in respect of which evidence has been supplied in relation to paragraph (2) which might affect compliance with the requirements of this Chapter.

(5) Any report or notification to the licensing authority under paragraph (2) or (4) must be accompanied by the appropriate fee in accordance with the Fees Regulations.

(6) The licensing authority may give a notice to a registered broker requiring that broker to provide information of a kind specified in the notice within the period specified in the notice.

(7) A notice under paragraph (6) may not be given to a registered broker unless it appears to the licensing authority that it is necessary for the licensing authority to consider whether the registration should be varied, suspended or revoked.

(8) A notice under paragraph (6) may specify information which the licensing authority thinks necessary for considering whether the registration should be varied, suspended or revoked.

(9) In paragraph (3)(b), "reporting year" means a period of twelve months ending on 31st March.

Glossary of Legislation

Contents

European Legislation

Council Directive 2001/83/EC on the Community code relating to medicinal products for human use

This legislation regulates the licensing, manufacture of and wholesale dealing in medicinal products and registration, brokering of medicinal products and manufacture, importation and distribution of active substances within the European Community.

UK Legislation

The Human Medicines Regulations 2012 (SI 2012/1916)

The Regulations set out a comprehensive regime for the authorisation of medicinal products for human use; for the manufacture, import, distribution, sale and supply of those products; for their labelling and advertising; and for pharmacovigilance.

For the most part the Regulations implement Directive 2001/83/EC of the European Parliament and of the Council of 6 November 2001 on the community code relating to medicinal products for human use (as amended). They also provide for the enforcement in the United Kingdom of Regulation (EC) No 726/2004 laying down Community procedures for the authorisation and supervision of medicinal products for human and veterinary use and establishing a European Medicines Agency.

These Regulations consolidate the 1968 Medicines Act and its supporting regulations including:

- **The Medicines (Applications for Manufacturer's and Wholesale Dealer's Licences) Regulations 1971 (SI 1971 No. 974), as amended**

- Medicines (Manufacturer's Undertakings for Imported Products) Regulations 1977 (SI 1977 No. 1038), as amended
- Medicines for Human Use (Marketing Authorisations Etc.) Regulations 1994 (SI 1994 No. 3144), as amended
- Prescription Only Medicines (Human Use) Order 1997 (as amended) (SI 1997 No. 1830), as amended

The Medicines (Products for Human Use) (Fees) Regulations 2013 (2013 No. 532)

These Regulations make provision for the fees payable under the Medicines Act 1971 in respect of marketing authorizations, licences and certificates relating to medicinal products for human use.

The Medicines for Human Use (Clinical Trials) Regulations 2004 (SI 2004 No. 1031) as amended

These Regulations implement Directive 2001/20/EC on the approximation of laws, regulations and administrative provisions of the Member States relating to the implementation of good clinical practice in the conduct of clinical trials on medicinal products for human use.

The Unlicensed Medicinal Products for Human Use (Transmissible Spongiform Encephalopathies) (Safety) Regulations 2003 (SI 2003 No. 1680)

Regulates the importation and marketing of unlicensed medicinal products for human use in order to minimise the risk of the transmission of Transmissible Spongiform Encephalopathies via those products.

Appendix

Human and Veterinary Medicines Authorities in Europe

AGES Medizinmarktaufsicht–Bundesamt für
Sicherheit im Gesundheitswesen
Traisengasse 5
A-1200 Wien
Austria
Website(s)   www.basg.gv.at

Federal Agency for Medicines and Health
Products
EUROSTATION building,
block 2 place Victor Horta,
40/ 40
1060 Brussels
Belgium
Email   welcome@fagg-afmps.be
Website(s)   www.fagg-afmps.be/en/

Bulgarian Drug Agency
26, Yanko Sakazov Blvd
1504 Sofia
Bulgaria
Phone   +359 2 943 40 46
Fax   +359 2 943 44 87
Email   bda@bda.bg
Website(s)   www.bda.bg

Ministry of Health Pharmaceutical Services
7 Larnacos Avenue
CY - 1475 Nicosia
Cyprus
Website(s)   http://www.moh.gov.cy

State Institute for Drug Control
Srobárova 48
CZ - 100 41 Praha 10
Czech Republic
Website(s)   www.sukl.cz/enindex.htm

Danish Health and Medicines Agency
Axel Heides Gade 1
DK – 2300 København S
Denmark
Phone   +45 72 22 74 00
Fax   +45 44 88 95 99
Email   sst@sst.dk
Website(s)   www.dkma.dk

State Agency of Medicines
1 Nooruse Street
EE-50411 Tartu
Estonia
Phone   +372 737 41 40
Fax   +372 737 41 42
Email   sam@sam.ee
Website(s)   www.sam.ee/

Finnish Medicines Agency
Mannerheimintie 103b
FIN – 00301 Helsinki
Finland
Phone   +358 9 473 341
Fax   +358 9 714 469
Website(s)   www.fimea.fi/

Agence nationale de sécurité
du médicament et des
produits de santé (ANSM)
143-147 bd Anatole France
FR-93285 Saint Denis Cedex
France
Website(s)   www.ansm.sante.fr

BfArM
Kurt-Georg-Kiesinger-Allee 3
53175 Bonn
Germany
Phone   +49 (0)228-207-30
Fax   +49 (0)228-207-5207
Email   info@bfarm.de
Website(s) www.bfarm.de

Paul-Ehrlich Institut
Paul-Ehrlich-Straße 51-59
63225 Langen
Germany
Phone   +49 6103 77 0
Fax   +49 6103 77 1234
Email   pei@pei.de
Website(s) www.pei.de
(Vaccine, Blood Products, Sera)

National Organization for Medicines
Messogion Avenue 284
GR – 15562 Athens
Greece
Phone   +30 210 6507200
Fax   +30 210 6545535
Email   relation@eof.gr
Website(s) www.eof.gr/
(Pharmaceuticals and Immunologicals)

National Institute of Pharmacy
Zrínyi U. 3
H-1051 Budapest
Hungary
Website(s) www.ogyi.hu/

Icelandic Medicines Agency
Vinlandsleid 14
IS – 113 Reykjavik
Iceland
Phone   +354 520 2100
Fax   +354 561 2170
Email   ima@ima.is
Website(s) www.ima.is

Irish Medicines Board
Kevin O'Malley House, The Earlsfort Centre,
Earlsfort Terrace
IRL – Dublin 2 Dublin
Ireland
Phone   +353 1 676 4971
Fax   +353 1 676 7836
Email   imb@imb.ie
Website(s) www.imb.ie/

Agenzia Italiana del Farmaco
Via del Tritone, 181
I-00187 Roma
Italy
Phone   +39 6 5978401
Fax   +39 6 59944142
Email   forenamefirstletter.surname@
           aifa.gov.it
Website(s) www.agenziafarmaco.it/

Ministero della Salute,
Direzione Generale della
Sanità Pubblica Veterinaria,
degli Allimenti e della Nutrizione, Uff. XI
Piazzale G. Marconi 25
I – 00144 Roma
Italy
Phone   +39 06 59 94 65 84
Fax   +39 06 59 94 69 49
Website(s) www.ministerosalute.it/

State Agency of Medicines of Latvia
15 Jersikas Street
LV – 1003 Riga
Latvia
Phone   +371-7078424
Fax   +371-7078428
Email   info@zva.gov.lv
Website(s) www.zva.gov.lv/

Office of Health/Dpt. of Pharmaceuticals
Äulestr 512
FL – 9490 Vaduz
Liechtenstein
Website(s) www.llv.li/

State Medicines Control Agency
Žirmūnų str. 139A
LT-09120 Vilnius
Lithuania
Website(s) www.vvkt.lt/

Direction de la Santé Villa
Louvigny Division de la
Pharmacie et des
Medicaments
Allée Marconi
L - 2120 Luxembourg
Luxembourg
Email   Ministere-Sante@ms.etat.lu
Website(s) www.ms.etat.lu

Medicines Authority
203, Level 3, Rue D´Argens
GZR 1368 Gzira
Malta
Phone   +356 23439000
Fax   +356 23439161
Email   info.medicinesauthority@gov.mt
Website(s) www.medicinesauthority.gov.mt

College ter Beoordeling van
Geneesmiddelen Medicines
Evaluation Board
Graadt van Roggenweg 500
NL - 3531 AH Utrecht
The Netherlands
Phone   +31 (0) 88 - 224 80 00
Fax   +31 (0) 88 - 224 80 01
Email   info@cbg-meb.nl
Website(s) www.cbg-meb.nl/

The Norwegian Medicines Agency
Sven Oftedalsvei 6
N- 0950 Oslo
Norway
Phone   +47 22 89 77 00
Fax   +47 22 89 77 99
Email   post@legemiddelverket.no
Website(s) www.legemiddelverket.no

Office for Registration of Medicinal Products,
Medical Devices and Biocidal Products
41 Zabkowska Str.
03-736 Warsaw
Poland
+48 (22) 492 11 00
+48 (22) 492 11 09
Website(s) bip.urpl.gov.pl

INFARMED – Instituto
Nacional da Farmácia e do
Medicamento Parque da
Saúde de Lisboa
Av. do Brasil 53
P –1749-004 Lisboa
Portugal
Phone   +351 217987100
Fax   +351 217987316
Email   infarmed@infarmed.pt
Website(s) www.infarmed.pt/portal/page/
portal/INFARMED

National Medicines Agency
48, Av. Sanatescu
011478 Bucharest
Romania
Phone   +4021 3171100
Fax   +4021 3163497
Website(s) www.anm.ro/en/home.html

State Institute for Drug Control
Kvetná 11
SK-825 08 Bratislava 26
Slovakia
Phone   +421 2 5070 1111
Fax   +421 2 5556 4127
Email   sukl@sukl.sk
Website(s) www.sukl.sk/

Javna agencija Republike
Slovenije za zdravila in
medicinske pripomočke
Ptujska ulica 21
Sl-1000 Ljubljana
Slovenia
Phone   + 38 6 8 2000 500
Fax   + 38 6 8 2000 510
Email   info@jazmp.si
Website(s) www.jazmp.si

Agencia Española de Medicamentos y Productos
Sanitarios
Parque Empresarial Las
Mercedes Edificio 8C/.
Campezo, 1
E - 28022 Madrid
Spain
Website(s) www.agemed.es

Medical Products Agency
Dag Hammarskjölds väg 42 / Box 26
SE – 751 03 UPPSALA
Sweden
Phone   +46 (0) 18 17 46 00
Fax   +46 (0) 18 54 85 66
Email   registrator@mpa.se
Website(s)   www.lakemedelsverket.se

DG Enterprise and Industry – F/2 BREY 10/073
Avenue d'Auderghem 45
B – 1049 Brussels
Belgium

EOF – National Drug Organisation
Messogion Street 284
GR – 15562 Athens
Greece

European Commission, DG Enterprise F2 Pharmaceuticals
Rue de la Loi 200
B-1049 Bruxelles
Belgium

European Medicines Agency (EMA)
7 Westferry Circus
E14 4HB London
United Kingdom
Phone   +44 20 74 18 84 00
Fax   +44 20 74 18 84 16
Email   info@ema.europa.eu
Website(s)   www.ema.europa.eu/

Index